ST GEORGE'S CHAPEL WINDSOR CASTLE

AN ILLUSTRATED HISTORY

Garter banners in the Quire

ST GEORGE'S CHAPEL WINDSOR CASTLE

AN ILLUSTRATED HISTORY

Clare Rider MA, PhD, DAA, FSA

2017

Second edition 2023

ISBN 978-0-9539676-5-0

Printed and bound by Short Run Press Ltd, Exeter

Contents

Statue of St George, carved in the 15th century. Formerly on a screen in the Quire, it was removed in the 20th century and is now housed in the Vicars' Hall Undercroft

PICTURE ACKNOWLEDGEMENTS

Front cover, pages ii, vi, xii, 3 (both), 12, 18, 20, 21 (bottom), 22 (both), 24 (bottom), 26, 27, 35, 40, 41 (top), 44, 49, 51, 55, 60, 64 (top and bottom right), 65, 67 (both), 82 (bottom), 85, 85, 88: John Crook © John Crook;

pages viii, x, 14 (bottom), 16, 28: John Crook © Country Life/John Crook;

page 1: Bibliotheque Nationale, Paris © Bibliotheque Nationale, Paris, France/Bridgeman Images;

pages 2 (top), **8**: British Library, London, UK © British Library Board. All Rights Reserved/ Bridgeman Images;

pages 2 (bottom), 11: Rena Gardiner watercolours reproduced with permission from the Gardiner estate;

pages 5, 6, 7, 14 (top), 17, 29, 33, 34, 36, 37, 41 (bottom), 42, 46, 47, 54, 56, 57, 63, 68 (bottom), 89, 92 (top): Doug Harding © Dean and Canons of Windsor;

page 9: ©Eton College. Reproduced by permission of the Provost and Fellows of Eton College;

pages 10 (b-d); 13, 52: Doug Harding © Dean and Canons of Windsor/Doug Harding;

pages 10 (top), 19 (top), 23 (top), 31 (bottom), 84 (right): Charlotte Manley © Dean and Canons of Windsor;

pages 19 (bottom), 30 (bottom), 32(top), 53, 59, 76 (bottom), 84 (left): Richard Shellabear © Dean and Canons of Windsor/ Royal Collection Trust;

pages 23 (bottom), 24 (top), 38: Angelo Hornak © Dean and Canons of Windsor;

pages 25, 62, 76 (bottom): Ivan Parr © Dean and Canons of Windsor;

pages 30 (top), 32 (bottom), 39: Eva Zielinska-Millar © Dean and Canons of Windsor;

page 36 (bottom): Peter Miles © Dean and Canons of Windsor;

page 43: British Museum, London UK © Trustees of the British Museum;

pages 45, 77, 91: David Clare © David Clare;

pages 48, 68 (top), 69: George Spearman © Dean and Canons of Windsor;

page 50: National Portrait Gallery, London, UK © National Portrait Gallery, London;

page 66: Royal Collection Trust/© Her Majesty Queen Elizabeth II 2017

page 70: National Portrait Gallery, London, UK © National Portrait Gallery, London;

page 82 (top): © Central Press Agency;

page 83: © Keystone Press;

page 87: © Windsor & Eton Express;

page 90: Crown Copyright

page 92: © Charlotte Burn Photography;

page 94, 95: © Press Association;

page 96: © Gill Heppell;

Other images © The Dean and Canons of Windsor

Foreword

St George's Chapel has been at the heart of the College of St George, Windsor Castle, since its foundation by King Edward III in 1348. The present Chapel, begun by King Edward IV in 1475, is a wonderful building, combining magnificent architecture and artistic achievement, and enriching our understanding of a long and interesting history. For more than 500 years, it has been the spiritual home of the Most Noble Order of the Garter, the most prestigious chivalric order in the world, and has served as a place of worship for members of the Royal Family, for those who live and work in Windsor Castle, and for our many visitors.

I have very much valued the opportunity to read this excellent new illustrated history, written by our Archivist and Chapter Librarian, Dr Clare Rider. I hope that it will deepen your knowledge of St George's Chapel, increase your understanding of its past, and enhance your appreciation of its splendour. I hope too that it will give you a sense of its being a building that is loved and cherished; one in which God's praises continue to be sung every day.

David Conner, *Dean of Windsor*

Portrait of Harry William Blackburne (Canon of Windsor 1931–34; Dean of Bristol 1934–51), author of *The Romance of St George's Chapel, Windsor Castle* (1933). Drawn by Francis Dodd in 1934

Preface

In 1933, the Friends of St George's, Windsor, published *The Romance of St George's Chapel,* which had been compiled by Canon Blackburne for the interest and enjoyment of Chapel visitors. Subsequent editions, revised by Maurice Bond, Honorary Custodian of the Muniments, and then by Peter Begent, historian and heraldic advisor to St George's Chapel, added greater academic and architectural content to the book. The final edition, the sixteenth, was published in 2001. By 2014, with stocks running low, the Dean and Canons decided to replace *The Romance* with a new publication. The result is this illustrated history. The Society of Friends of St George's and Descendants of the Knights of the Garter, who had funded the successive editions of *The Romance*, generously agreed to meet the publication costs. As in the past, all profits received from sales of the publication will be used by the Dean and Canons to assist in the preservation and maintenance of the Chapel and its heritage.

As author, I should like to record my gratitude to the Dean and Canons, the Friends and Descendants and all those others who have contributed in any way to the production of this history, from its conception, through its design, writing, illustration and editing, to its publication. Particular thanks are due to fellow members of the Publications Sub-Committee (Canon Mark Powell, Charlotte Manley, John Crook and Bridget Wright); to Kate McQuillian, Enid Davies, Anastasia Porteous and other members of the Archives Team; to Tim Tatton-Brown, who read and commented on the text; to the photographers whose skills contribute so much to the appearance of the book (in particular John Crook, Doug Harding, Richard Shellabear and Charlotte Manley); to Jill Atherton for her meticulously drawn Chapel plan; and to Paul Luffman and his colleagues at Short Run Press for their advice and support as well as for producing a publication of such high quality. For any errors or shortcomings which remain, *mea culpa.*

Clare Rider, *Archivist and Chapter Librarian*

Fig 1.1 The Aerary Porch, built between 1353 and 1354 as the main entrance to Edward III's new College of St George

CHAPTER ONE

Beginnings
Edward III and the Foundation of the College of St George

The College of St George was founded by Edward III (1327–1377) on 6 August 1348. Following his victory over the French at the Battle of Crécy in 1346, the King's military reputation was at its height, with his popularity further increased by rising prosperity and political stability at home.

Fig 1.2 The Battle of Crécy, 1346, from *Chronique d'Angleterre*, Bibliotheque Nationale Fr 87 f.117

To acknowledge his gratitude and devotion to God, he decided to found religious establishments within two of his favourite royal residences: Windsor Castle (where he had been born in 1312) and Westminster Palace. These royal foundations, dedicated respectively to St George and St Stephen, were early examples of a new type of religious institution – the secular college – a community of clergy and lay people living together without taking monastic vows. Their common purpose was to thank God for past successes and to pray for the future well-being of the souls of the King, his ancestors and successors. Edward III obtained formal approval for the foundation of his new Royal Colleges from Pope Clement VI and, in 1351, secured the Pope's permission to establish them as 'peculiars', exempt from the jurisdiction of the traditional Church authorities. The 'King's Free Chapels' of St George and St Stephen were to be governed under statutes drawn up by the authority of the Pope and supervised by the Lord Chancellor of England. They were not accountable to the Archbishop of Canterbury or to the bishops of their local dioceses.

Fig 1.3 Edward III from 'William Bruges' Garter Book' c.1450, English School, British Library Stowe MS 594 f.7v

The College at Windsor Castle was to have an additional and distinctive role: to serve as the spiritual home of the King's newly founded Company of the Garter, a chivalric fraternity or brotherhood based at Windsor which survives to this day as the Most Noble Order of the Garter. In restricting membership to the Sovereign, his son Edward (known as The Black Prince) and an élite of twenty-four knights, Edward III was able to reward the faithful service of these knights in battle and, he hoped, secure their future loyalty.

There was no need to build a new chapel at Windsor: Edward III was able to grant the Royal Chapel, constructed by Henry III (1216–1272) in the Lower Ward of Windsor Castle, to the College. The beautiful red and gold Gilebertus doors at the east end of the present Chapel are survivors of this thirteenth-century building (Fig 1.5). Originally dedicated to St Edward the Confessor, the Chapel was rededicated, on the College's foundation in 1348, 'to the honour of God Almighty, and of his mother, the glorious Virgin Mary, and

Fig 1.4 Watercolour reconstruction by Rena Gardiner of the procession to Henry III's Chapel at its consecration in 1249

Fig 1.5 13th century entrance to Henry III's Chapel with doors decorated with magnificent medieval ironwork by master-smith, Gilebertus, whose name is incorporated in the design, c.1240

of the Saints George the Martyr and Edward the Confessor'.[1] As the soldier saint became adopted as the patron of the Order of the Garter, the building became known as St George's Chapel.

The thirteenth-century building, on the site now occupied by the Albert Chapel, was a great deal smaller than its successor, the grand St George's Chapel which we know today. When it had been established by Henry III in the 1240s, it had been served by a small staff of Royal Chaplains. Edward III made significant alterations to the Chapel, inserting elaborately-carved wooden stalls for the Garter Knights and constructing a stone-vaulted vestry and a new entrance porch and passage-way to the north. He aimed to transform Henry

Fig 1.6 Canons' Cloister, photographed from the south-east corner. Constructed between 1350 and 1357, it has undergone many alterations, including the addition of a large extension into the garth in the late 15th century and the insertion of several external chimneys stacks. The west-side of the cloister was demolished and rebuilt in the 17th century

Fig 1.7 The treasury room, known as the Aerary, constructed between 1353 and 1355 to house the College's written records, money, jewels and other treasures. The wooden filing drawers, built in 1422 to house the property deeds and account rolls, were still in use for the storage of archives in 1956, when this photograph was taken

III's modest establishment into a prestigious ecclesiastical institution; a worthy spiritual home for his new chivalric fraternity.

The King's original intention, expressed in the College's foundation document of 6 August 1348, was to appoint a Warden and twenty-three Canons to serve and maintain the Chapel. However, the outbreak of the Black Death in 1348–49 delayed the implementation of the King's plans. By the time the College Statutes were issued in 1352, the number of Canons had been reduced to twelve. The Warden and Canons were to be assisted by thirteen minor clergy, known as Priest Vicars, four choirmen, known as Lay Clerks, six Choristers and a Virger, who together were responsible for celebrating choral services in the Chapel.

Edward III intended that the College of St George should be completed by the appointment of twenty-six retired soldiers, described in the Statutes as 'Poor Knights', who were to receive accommodation and a living allowance in return for their daily prayers for the King and Knights of the Garter. However, because of financial constraints, only one, two or three Poor Knights were in post at any one time during the Middle Ages.

In addition to the Royal Chapel, Edward III gave the land surrounding it to the newly-founded College, together with the other royal buildings constructed in the Lower Ward by Henry II and Henry III. He also paid for the construction of houses for the accommodation of the resident members of the College – the present Deanery and Canons' Cloister houses (Fig 1.6), which date from the 1350s. A grand new stone-vaulted entrance porch (Fig 1.1), with a treasury room (known as the Aerary) above it (Fig 1.7), completed the collegiate buildings.

Edward III also donated properties within the town of Windsor and elsewhere in England, to produce a regular income to maintain the establishment. These grants, which included the manors of Bray, in Berkshire, and Iver, in Buckinghamshire, were increased by donations from the founder Knights of the Garter, including a substantial gift from the Black Prince of property in Saltash, Cornwall.

However, not all the revenue sources promised by the King materialised and the College struggled financially until its income was supplemented by the generosity of private benefactors, who granted material possessions to the Warden and Canons in return for the spiritual benefit of prayers for their souls. Foremost amongst these was John, Duke of Bedford, brother of Henry V, who enriched the College with the grant in 1421 of many of the 'spiritualities' (church properties and revenues) formerly belonging to Ogbourne Priory. These included the rectories of Glynde in Sussex, Hungerford in Berkshire and Ruislip in Middlesex and tithes from Tooting Bec, then in Surrey, Whitchurch in Oxfordshire, and Waddesdon in Buckinghamshire.

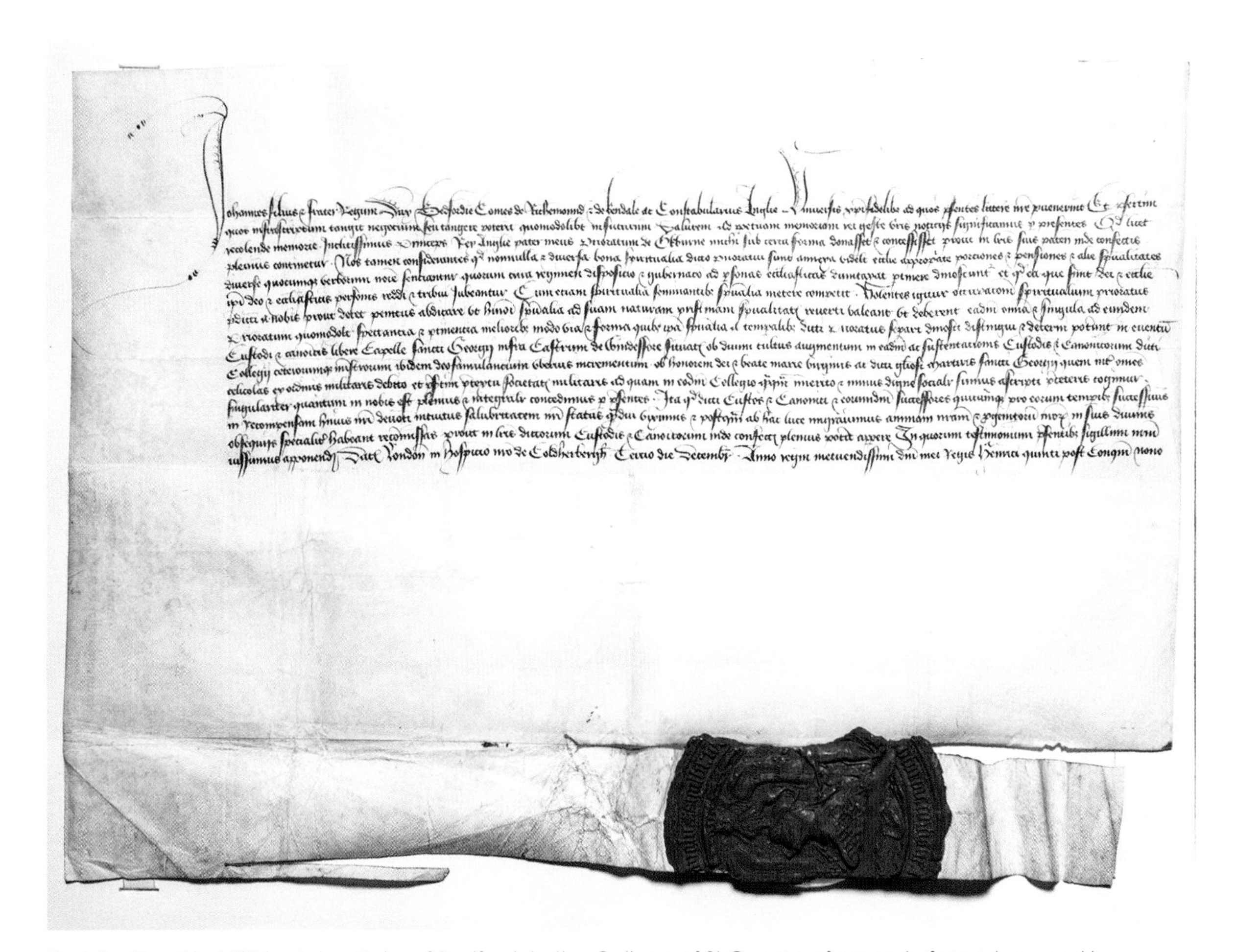

Fig 1.8 Grant in 1421 by John, Duke of Bedford, to the College of St George of property formerly owned by Ogbourne Priory

Fig 2.1 The Vicars' Hall, built or adapted from a previous building in about 1415

CHAPTER TWO

Consolidation The later Plantagenets and the House of Lancaster

During the reigns of Edward III's immediate successors, daily services continued in Henry III's former Chapel. Garter ceremonies were held annually, usually from 22 to 24 April, and included a Garter Feast on St George's Day (23 April), a Thanksgiving Service and a Memorial Mass for past Knights. These were generally celebrated at Windsor, but could be held elsewhere, unless they included the installation of new Garter Knights, which could take place only at St George's Chapel, where the Garter stalls were located.

Meanwhile, the Warden (known as the Dean from the fifteenth century), Canons, Priest Vicars, Lay Clerks, Choristers and Poor Knights continued to pray every day for the King, the Knights of the Garter and 'all Christian souls' as instructed by their founder. A register for 1384–1385 records those who attended the eight services of Divine Office (Mattins, Lauds, Prime, Terce, Sext, None, Vespers and Compline). In addition there might be three or more daily Masses.

This gruelling schedule was clearly too demanding for some. An official visitation in October 1384, during the reign of Richard II (1377–99), revealed flaws in attendance and prompted the keeping of the register mentioned

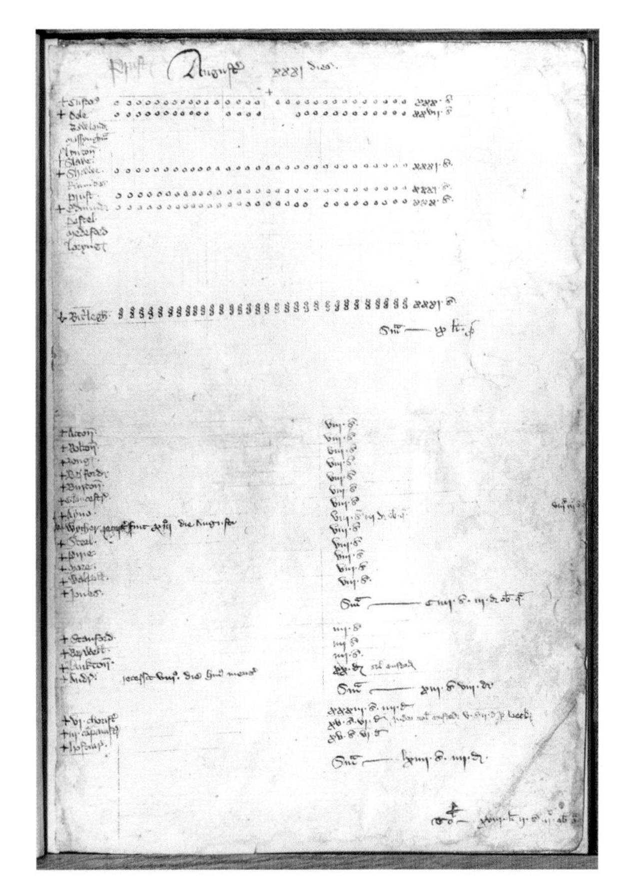

Fig 2.2 Page from an attendance register commenced in October 1384, following an official visitation of the College. The register records the allowances paid to the Custos (Warden), Canons, Vicars, Poor Knights, Lay Clerks, Choristers, Bell-ringers and Virger

Fig 2.3 Portrait of Geoffrey Chaucer c.1415–1420 from Thomas Hoccleve's *Regiment of Princes*, British Library Harleian MS. 4866 f.88

above, which survives in the Chapel archives (Fig 2.2). However, further inspections in 1408 and 1434 showed that the problem of poor attendance had not been resolved.

In Richard II's reign the Chapel fabric caused concern. In 1390, Geoffrey Chaucer, Clerk of Works at Windsor Castle but better known as the author of *The Canterbury Tales*, was commissioned to repair St George's Chapel, which was in a condition 'which threatens ruin and is in danger of falling to the ground unless it be speedily and effectually repaired'.[2] Chaucer was authorised 'to impress masons, carpenters and other workmen at the King's wages, to requisition materials of every description and carriages for their conveyance and to imprison refractory persons' who objected to the forced levy.[3]

Repairs and alterations continued in the reign of Richard II's successor, Henry IV (1399–1413), whose attention also turned to the College's domestic buildings. In 1409 the King granted the Dean and Canons additional land in the Lower Ward (known as Woodhawe) on which to build extra accommodation for the Priest Vicars, Clerks and Choristers. The building works, which took place several years later, between 1415 and 1416, included the construction or conversion of an existing building into a hall for the Priest Vicars, a communal meeting place which still bears their name (Fig 2.1).

Henry V (1413–22) and Henry VI (1422–61; 1470–71) installed Garter Knights at Windsor but otherwise showed little interest in the Chapel. Indeed, Henry VI's own grand building scheme – the construction of Eton College across the river from Windsor – diverted royal attention and resources away from St George's Chapel.

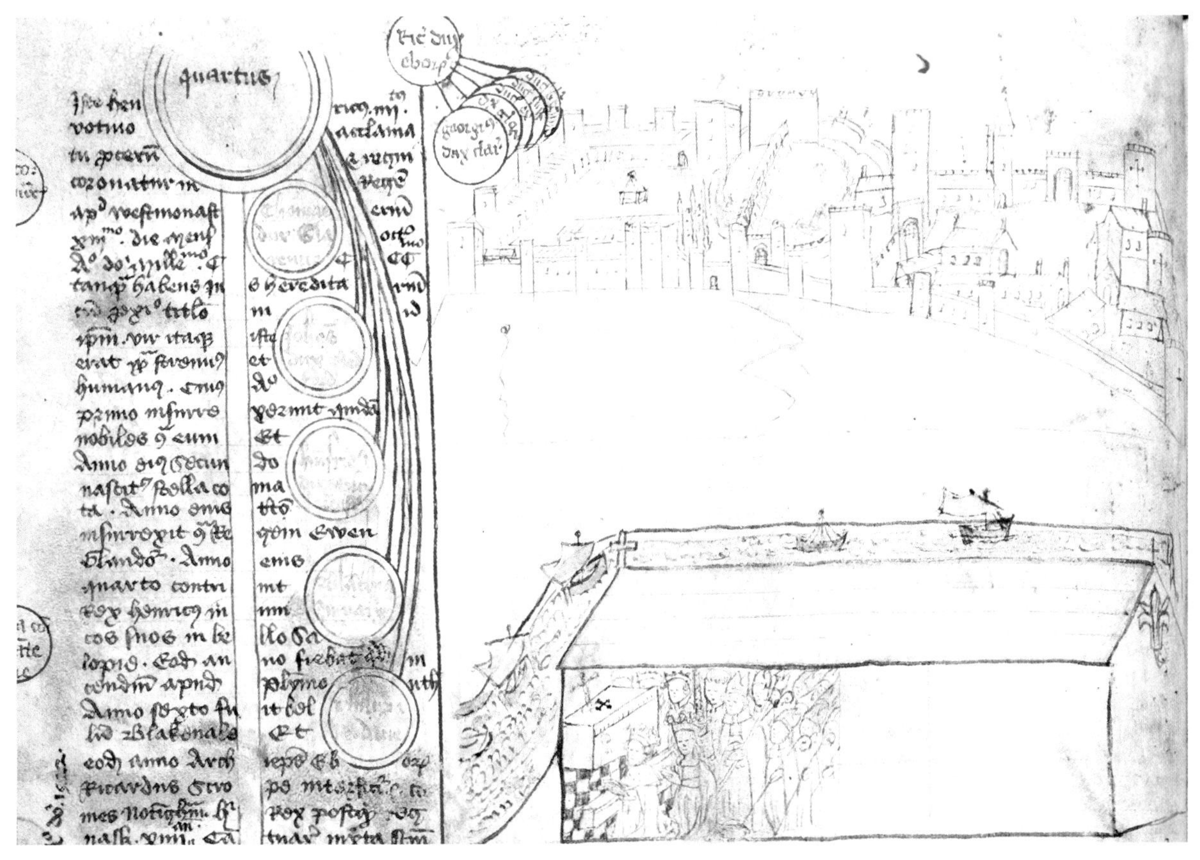

Fig 2.4 Drawing of Henry VI praying in his newly-founded College at Eton, with Windsor Castle in the background, in a manuscript of Ranulf Higden's *Polychronicon*, c.1450, Eton College MS 213

Fig 3.1a Popey in the Quire carved with the Crucifixion scene

Fig 3.1b Misericord, featuring a human figure and four eagles

Fig 3.1c Lower elbow of a stall, depicting an ape in a monk's habit

Fig 3.1d Upper elbow of a stall, depicting curled-up dra

CHAPTER THREE

Growth
The Yorkists and the New St George's Chapel

Circumstances were to change in the reign of Henry VI's rival and successor, Edward IV (1461–1470; 1471–1483). Having emerged victorious from the rigours of civil war (later known as 'The Wars of the Roses'), during which he distinguished himself in battle, Edward IV wished to thank God for his past successes, to ensure the future well-being of the royal dynasty and to create a mausoleum at Windsor for the House of York. To fulfil these aims he ordered the construction of a new Royal Chapel at Windsor to the west of the existing Chapel. It was to be a building of exceptional size and grandeur, to provide a worthy resting-place for himself and his family and to outdo Henry VI's uncompleted chapel at Eton.

On 19 February 1473 he appointed Richard

Fig 3.2 Watercolour reconstruction by Rena Gardiner of Edward IV's new St George's Chapel under construction in the 15th century

Beauchamp, Bishop of Salisbury, as Master and Surveyor of Works for the new Chapel. Two years later, in 1475, orders were given for a very large area to the west of the old Chapel to be cleared to enable building work to commence.

With the able assistance of master-mason Henry Janyns, who had previously worked at Eton College, wood-carver William Berkeley, iron-smith John Tresilian, and Clerk of Works Thomas Canceller, Bishop Beauchamp set about the construction of a magnificent new chapel.

The Bishop had proved himself an able Surveyor of Works at Salisbury, overseeing an extensive refurbishment of the Cathedral and the Bishop's Palace there. At Windsor, he was authorised to employ all the craftsmen and labourers he needed for the new work and to requisition materials and carts. Yellow freestone was brought by land and river from quarries to the west of Burford, Reigate stone from wharfs in London and timber from the neighbouring villages of Upton, Farnham and Sunninghill. Hundreds of craftsmen were brought in to work on St George's Chapel; indeed so many stone-cutters were employed at Windsor in 1478 that Oxford University had difficulty finding sufficient skilled workmen to finish the Divinity Schools there.

Several buildings on the western part of the site, including the offices of the Royal Almonry, were demolished to lay foundations for the Nave and to construct a new cloister (the Horseshoe Cloister) to house the minor clergy and choirmen. Appointed Dean of Windsor in 1478, Bishop Beauchamp was the driving force behind the initial stages of the building project and continued to supervise it closely until his death in 1481.

During the remainder of Edward IV's reign, work continued in earnest at the east end of the new Chapel, the first part to be fitted with a vaulted stone roof. The Quire was furnished with elaborately-decorated wooden stalls for the Knights of the Garter and the Clergy, which were carved and installed under the direction of William Berkeley between 1477 and 1484. The quality of craftsmanship of this woodwork is exceptional (Fig 3.1a-d). The finials at the desk ends (known as popeys) include illustrations of the lives of St George the Martyr and of the Virgin Mary, and the

Fig 3.3 John Tresilian's ironwork gates for Edward IV's tomb, 1478. Originally in the North Quire Aisle, they were moved to their present position by the High Altar in 1789

Fig 3.4 Sovereign's seat misericord depicting Edward IV securing a treaty with Louis XI of France at Picquigny in 1475

story of Christ's Passion. The carvings on the misericords on the underside of the seats include secular as well as religious scenes and designs. Recent research suggests that many were inspired by German and Flemish prints.

Under the Sovereign's stall is a spectacular misericord, which must have been commissioned directly by Edward IV (Fig 3.4). It depicts his diplomatic victory over the French, with the securing of a favourable peace treaty with the King of France, Louis XI, at Picquigny in 1475. As a result of this treaty, Edward IV received a substantial annual pension from the French King, which played a major part in financing the construction of the Chapel.

When Edward IV died in 1483, the Chapel was ready to receive his mortal remains, which were buried in a vault on the north side of the Quire, close to the High Altar and directly below his Chantry Chapel over the North Quire Aisle. His touchstone tomb, although not fully completed, was enclosed by Tresilian's intricately fashioned iron gates, the finest example of mediaeval ironwork to survive in the British Isles.

Edward IV had spent over £7,000 on the first phase of construction, an enormous sum in the fifteenth century. He and his Queen Consort, Elizabeth Woodville, also endowed the College with much additional property to maintain the building and the collegiate establishment, which was increased by the appointment of two Chantry Priests to say prayers for their souls and by the augmentation of the choir. The King donated the estates of St Anthony's Hospital in London, as well as lands and rectories stretching from Devon to Yorkshire; whilst the Queen's substantial gifts included the prosperous manors of Great Haseley and Puriton in Oxfordshire and Bassetsbury in Buckinghamshire, as well as an annual rent from the town of High Wycombe (Fig 3.5). These royal grants were supplemented by estates in Surrey, Berkshire and Hampshire formerly owned by the Priory of Sandleford, which were donated to the College by Sir Richard Beauchamp, nephew of Bishop Beauchamp.

Further benefactions were received from the founders of chantries in the new Chapel, including Sir Thomas St Leger and William, Lord Hastings, who granted property in return for the spiritual benefit of prayers for themselves and their families.

Edward IV arranged for holy relics to be transferred to the new Chapel to increase its spiritual status and to encourage pilgrims, whose offerings would contribute to the income of the College. The first and foremost

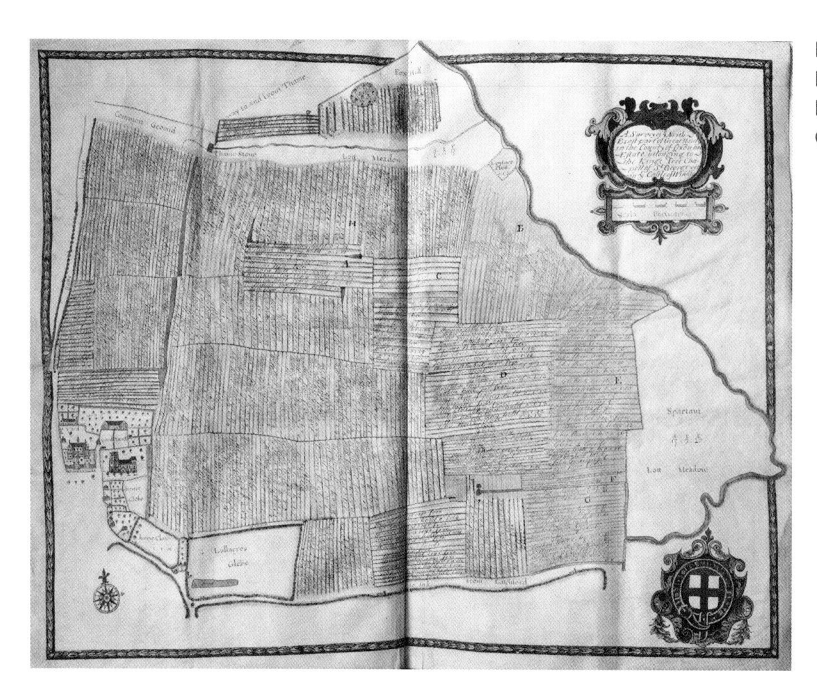

Fig 3.5 1729 survey plan by William Burgess of the manor of Great Haseley, Oxfordshire, granted to the College by Elizabeth Woodville in 1478

Fig 3.6 Roof-boss in the South Quire Aisle illustrating Edward IV and Bishop Beauchamp praying at the foot of the Cross Gneth, c.1480

of these was the Cross Gneth, said to be a piece of the cross on which Jesus Christ had died, which was housed in a highly ornamented and gilded container (known as a reliquary), fashioned in the shape of a Celtic cross. This relic had been captured by Edward I from Llewelyn, Prince of Wales, and had been given to St George's Chapel by Edward III. Edward IV had it moved to a shrine at the east end of the new Chapel. Destroyed at the time of the Protestant Reformation, the magnificent reliquary is commemorated in a roof-boss located immediately above the former shrine, which depicts Edward IV and Bishop Beauchamp praying at the foot of a golden Celtic cross. Nearby, the Bishop installed a stone niche, with an inscription, seeking prayers from those reading from the service book within it, whilst kneeling in the presence of the Holy Cross.

A further prestigious relic introduced into the new Chapel was acquired with some difficulty and considerable expenditure. This highly-prized object consisted of the bones of Master John Schorn, Rector of North Marston, Buckinghamshire, brought to Windsor in 1481, after negotiations involving the Pope and the Prior and Convent of Dunstable, Bedfordshire,

Fig 3.7 Replica pilgrim badge depicting John Schorn preaching from a pulpit, reproduced from an original in the Museum of London

as former owners of the Rectory of North Marston. Although never created a saint by the Church of Rome, John Schorn was widely venerated as a holy man, healer of the sick and miracle-worker both in his lifetime and after his death in 1313.

A chantry chapel was allocated to John Schorn at the south-east end of St George's Chapel, within which an elaborate shrine was constructed to house his remains. In the 1580s, when the veneration of relics had long ceased, the shrine was replaced by an alabaster tomb to commemorate the burial place of Edward, Earl of Lincoln, and his wife, Elizabeth. The Chapel of the Blessed John Schorn was thereafter known as the Lincoln Chapel.

Edward IV's younger brother, Richard III (1483–1485), added further to St George's

Fig 3.8 Monument to Edward, 1st Earl of Lincoln (died 1585) and his wife Elizabeth (died 1590) in the Lincoln Chapel, formerly the Chapel of the Blessed John Schorn

KING HENRY. VI
1422-1471

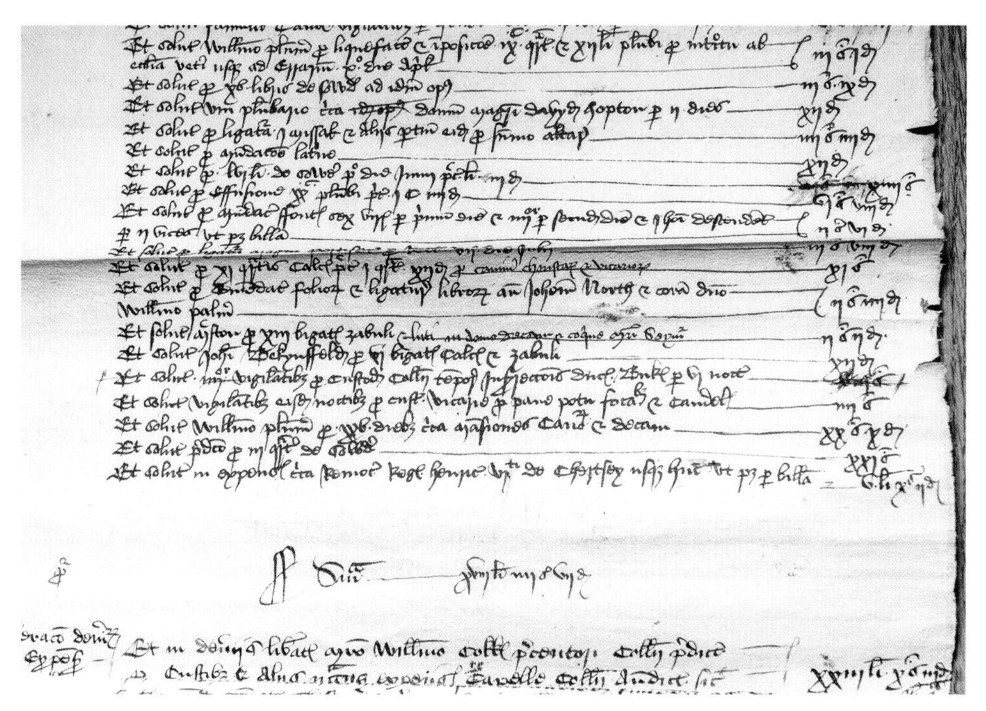

Fig 3.10 Cost of transporting the bones of Henry VI from Chertsey to Windsor in 1484 recorded in the Canon Treasurer's accounts as £5 10s 2d

Chapel's status as a site of pilgrimage by transporting the bones of Henry VI to Windsor from Chertsey Abbey, where they had rested since the death of the deposed King in 1471. Richard III's motivation for this action in 1484 is uncertain, unless he himself intended to be buried in the Chapel and wished to have the spiritual benefit of resting near the saintly King, whose relics were believed to be responsible for numerous miracles. Certainly pilgrims flocked to Windsor to the site of Henry VI's tomb in the South Quire Aisle. A fifteenth-century money box, designed and ornately executed by master-smith John Tresilian, stands beside the tomb awaiting the receipt of pilgrimage offerings.

When Richard III chose Westminster Abbey as the burial place of his wife, Anne Neville, in March 1485, Edward IV's dream of founding a Yorkist mausoleum at Windsor faded, even before the defeat of this, the last Yorkist King at the Battle of Bosworth in August 1485. Nevertheless, before his own death, Edward IV had laid the foundations of the magnificent Chapel, recognised today as one of the most distinguished buildings in Great Britain and served with one of the most accomplished choirs in the land. It was left to the Yorkists' successors, the Tudors, to complete this gem of artistic endeavour and spiritual aspiration.

◀ Fig 3.9 Henry VI's burial place to the south side of the High Altar. The iron money-box made by John Tresilian for pilgrims' offerings is in the foreground

Fig 4.1 The Nave looking west

CHAPTER FOUR

Completion
The Early Tudors

Henry VII (1485–1509), conscious of his tenuous claim to the throne of England and Wales, made every effort to consolidate his rule and to unite the kingdom under a strong government supported by the nobles of the realm. His marriage to Edward IV's daughter, Elizabeth of York, was a masterly stroke, bringing together the Houses of York and Lancaster to prevent future rivalry. Meanwhile, Henry VII made political use of the Order of the Garter to strengthen his position at Court. In addition to the traditional practice of appointing hereditary nobles as Knights of the Garter, he extended membership to some of the more humbly-born statesmen who had risen in his service, including Sir Thomas Lovell and Sir Reginald (or Reynold) Bray. In doing so, Henry VII brought men of very different backgrounds together, united by a pledge of loyalty. What better place could there be to celebrate the significance of this royal union and the prestige of the Order than in the Garter Chapel of St George?

The modern visitor to St George's Chapel, entering through the south door into the Nave and experiencing the splendour of the soaring stone-vaulting and the magnificence of the West Window, is viewing the building work completed by the Tudors.

Fig 4.2 Roof-boss depicting a Tudor rose within the Garter

Fig 4.3 'Consecration crosses' were carved into the walls of the new chapel to commemorate its consecration and celebrate its founder Edward IV. They depict a small image of Christ on the Cross imposed on the seeded centre of a double-petalled rose surrounded by sunbeams

At the time of Henry VII's accession to the throne, in August 1485, only the east end of the Chapel was nearing completion. According to Edward IV's wishes, the ceilings above his burial place and above the Cross Gneth shrine had been vaulted in beautiful carved honey-coloured Cotswold stone, decorated with roof bosses and intricate carvings on fine white stone imported from Caen in France. However, the Quire, which housed the magnificently-carved Garter stalls, remained to be vaulted, as did the west end of the North Quire Aisle.

The main body of the Chapel, including the Nave and Transepts, remained a shell. The north and south walls, carved with consecration crosses in the reign of Edward IV (Fig 4.3), reached only to window height. The west end had yet to be started. The Quire was in use for services, with a temporary roof and a partition and doorway dividing it from the unfinished Crossing and Nave, but much work remained to be done to complete Edward IV's vision.

In 1488 Henry VII participated in Garter Services in St George's Chapel and presided over the lavish ceremonies and a magnificent Garter Feast at Windsor, at which his Queen Consort, Elizabeth, and his mother, Lady Margaret Beaufort, were present, adorned in Garter robes. However, rather than completing Edward IV's new Chapel, Henry VII decided to concentrate his efforts and resources on a new project – constructing a new Lady Chapel to serve as a mausoleum for himself and his family, on the site of the original Garter Chapel (the site now occupied by the Albert Chapel).

Although the north and west walls of the thirteenth-century chapel were retained, the Lady Chapel was effectively a completely new building. In the centre was to be a glorious new shrine to the saintly Henry VI, whose remains were to be moved there from the South Quire Aisle, with Henry VII's own tomb beside it in a position of honour. Canon John Seymour oversaw the works, which continued from 1494 to 1498, at a cost of almost £5,000. The building was nearing completion when Henry VII had a change of mind. In 1498 the Abbot and Convent of Westminster petitioned the King, claiming the relics of Henry VI for Westminster Abbey, and, following a bitter dispute with the Dean and Canons of Windsor, the Privy Council decided in favour of Westminster Abbey.

Henry VII therefore abandoned building work at Windsor in order to construct a magnificent new Lady Chapel at the east end

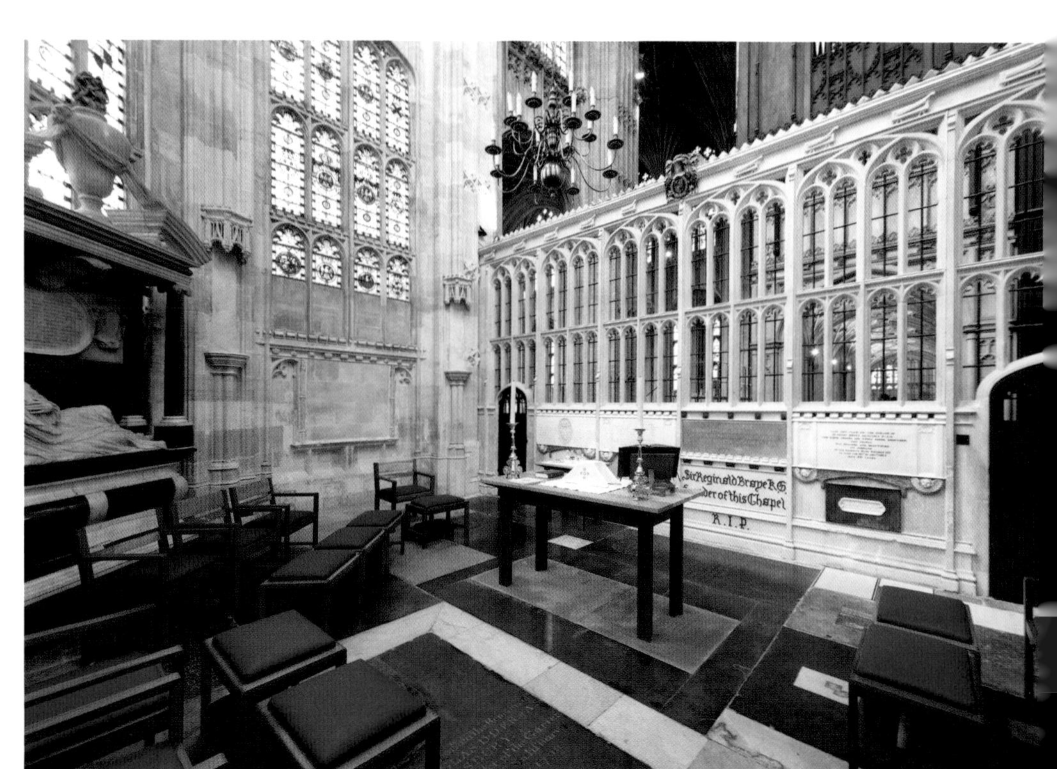

Fig 4.4 The Bray Chantry Chapel, constructed for Sir Reginald Bray (died 1503), prepared for a service in 2017

of Westminster Abbey where he planned to lie in splendour with the saintly King beside him. On Henry VII's death in 1509 he was, indeed, buried in a grand tomb within his Lady Chapel at Westminster. However, Henry VI's relics were not transferred from the South Quire Aisle in Windsor and remain there today.

Once Henry VII had abandoned his planned mausoleum at Windsor, building works gradually resumed in the main Chapel, almost certainly initiated by Christopher Urswick, (Canon 1492–96; Dean 1496–1505). In 1498, the west end of the North Quire Aisle vaulting was completed, and work recommenced on the Transepts. Urswick, who had come to Henry Tudor's notice as Chaplain to his mother, Lady Margaret Beaufort, was a familiar face at the Royal Court and served as the King's Chaplain

Fig 4.5 The Oliver King Chapel viewed from within, engraving by Orlando Jewitt from a drawing by C A Buckler

Fig 4.6 Memorial brass commemorating Anne, Duchess of Exeter (died 1476), sister of Edward IV, and her husband, Sir Thomas St Leger (died 1483), in the Rutland Chantry Chapel (originally named the Exeter Chantry Chapel)

and Confessor. He presided over the works at Windsor with the encouragement and financial backing of Henry VII's chief financial adviser, Sir Reginald (or Reynold) Bray, who had also risen in the service of Lady Margaret Beaufort, and of Oliver King, the King's Secretary and also a Canon of Windsor. As part of the works, Bray had a vast chantry chapel constructed in the South Transept to house his tomb (Fig 4.4).

At the same time, the Exeter Chantry Chapel on the north-side of the Crossing was completed in an almost identical style. This chantry had been founded by Thomas St Leger in 1481 for his wife, Edward IV's sister, Anne, Duchess of Exeter, who had died in childbirth in 1476. Their daughter, Anne, and her husband George Manners, Lord Roos, were subsequently buried in a magnificent alabaster tomb in the centre of the Chantry Chapel. It was renamed the Rutland Chantry Chapel after their son, Thomas Manners, had been created 1st Earl of Rutland by Henry VIII in 1525.

Meanwhile Oliver King (Canon of Windsor, 1480–1503) added a more modest chapel to the south-west corner of the South Quire Aisle,

Fig 4.7 Panels with portraits of the royal masters served by Oliver King (from right to left: Edward, son of Henry VI, Edward IV, Edward V and Henry VII) painted between 1492 and 1495

presumably intended as his place of burial (Fig 4.5). It is not known whether he was buried there on his death in 1503 or within the Diocese of Bath and Wells, where he held the Bishopric from 1495 to 1503. Opposite the Oliver King Chapel, a series of painted panels, dating from about 1492, portray the three Kings of England (Edward IV, Edward V and Henry VII) and the Prince of Wales (Edward, son of Henry VI) whom Oliver King served as Secretary.

Two small enclosed chantry chapels were constructed in the Quire Aisles: one, in the North Quire Aisle, in memory of William, Lord Hastings, Chamberlain to Edward IV (executed by Richard III in 1483), and the other, in the South Quire Aisle, to commemorate Canon John Oxenbridge (Canon 1509–1522).

Two side-chapels at the west end of the Nave were also converted into chantry chapels in the early-sixteenth century. The south-west one, now known as the Beaufort Chantry Chapel, was acquired in 1506 by Charles Somerset, Lord Herbert, an ancestor of the Dukes of Beaufort. The Urswick Chantry Chapel, on the north-west side, commemorates Dean Christopher Urswick, who retired in 1505 to the parish of Hackney, where he was buried after his death in 1522.

Fig 4.8 Carving above the door into the Urswick Chantry Chapel, featuring Urswick's coat of arms and a Tudor rose and portcullis supported by a red dragon and white greyhound in tribute to Henry VII

Fig 4.9 Hemp-bray on a roof boss in the South Nave Aisle commemorating Sir Reginald Bray, whose generous bequest funded the completion of the Nave

Fig 4.10 Hemp-bray on door lock on the Bray Chantry Chapel

Although occupied by a memorial to Princess Charlotte (Fig 9.5), the Urswick Chantry Chapel retains a stone screen with an inscription seeking prayers for the souls of Dean Urswick and of his patron, Henry VII. Above the door is an exquisite carving incorporating Henry VII's heraldic badges, the portcullis and the rose, supported by the red dragon and white greyhound, with Urswick's coat of arms (Fig 4.8).

The close relationship between Christopher Urswick, Oliver King and Reginald Bray, and their mutual interest in architecture, was not confined to Windsor. Records tell us that Urswick sent a gift of stone to Bray when he was constructing a grand new house at Eaton Bray in Bedfordshire and that Bray played a significant part in assisting Oliver King with advice and financial aid in his major project to rebuild Bath Abbey. Due to their joint enterprise, much work was undertaken on St George's Chapel in the 1490s. However, the main body of the Chapel might have remained unfinished for many decades had it not been for the generous bequest of Sir Reginald Bray on his death in 1503. One of the richest laymen in the land, having made his fortune in serving Henry VII, the childless Bray instructed his executors to provide sufficient funds to complete St George's Chapel according to its founder's original intention and design. In tribute to this exceptional patron, over 175 hemp-brays adorn the fabric of the finished Chapel, depicted in stone, wood, stained glass and ironwork, the hemp-bray (a device used in rope-making) being his heraldic badge (Figs 4.9-4.10).

William Vertue, one of the finest stonemasons in England, who had been working on Bray's Chantry Chapel and also on Henry VII's Lady Chapel at Westminster Abbey, was employed to complete and vault the Nave from 1503 to 1506. Although the King had not financed the work, it is likely that it was he who insisted on the inclusion of Tudor royal badges in the roof vaulting alongside the heraldic badges and coats of arms of the major benefactors, Reginald Bray and Christopher

Fig 4.12 Katherine of Aragon's oriel window in the Quire

Fig 4.11 The Quire looking east

Urswick. Certainly the subsequent contract for vaulting the Quire, which was agreed with William Vertue and John Hylmer in 1506, specified that the roof-bosses should be decorated with 'roses, portcullises, fleurs-de-lis and any other device that shall please the King's grace to have in them'.[4]

Whilst Sir Reginald Bray's bequest had financed the construction and vaulting of the Nave, it was left to the King and the Knights of the Garter to pay for the Quire vaulting. The heraldic badges of the Garter Knights alive when the vaulting was installed (1506–1509) may be seen on the roof-bosses which decorate the Quire, along with the royal badges chosen by Henry VII, and his successor, Henry VIII (1509–1547). Henry VIII's bosses included the initials H and K tied with a golden cord to celebrate his marriage with Katherine of Aragon in 1509. The Quire vault, with its low-rise and pendant bosses, is a masterpiece of design and execution. Edward IV's Chantry Chapel was converted into a royal closet, with the addition of a magnificently-decorated wooden oriel window, to enable Queen Katherine to view services and ceremonies in the Quire (Fig 4.12).

At about this time, carved-stone statues representing the King's heraldic beasts were installed on the pinnacles on the outside of the Chapel, where they remained until the seventeenth century. They were replaced with replicas in the 1920s (Fig 11.5).

Fig 4.13 Stone-mason figure in the West Window, possibly William Vertue

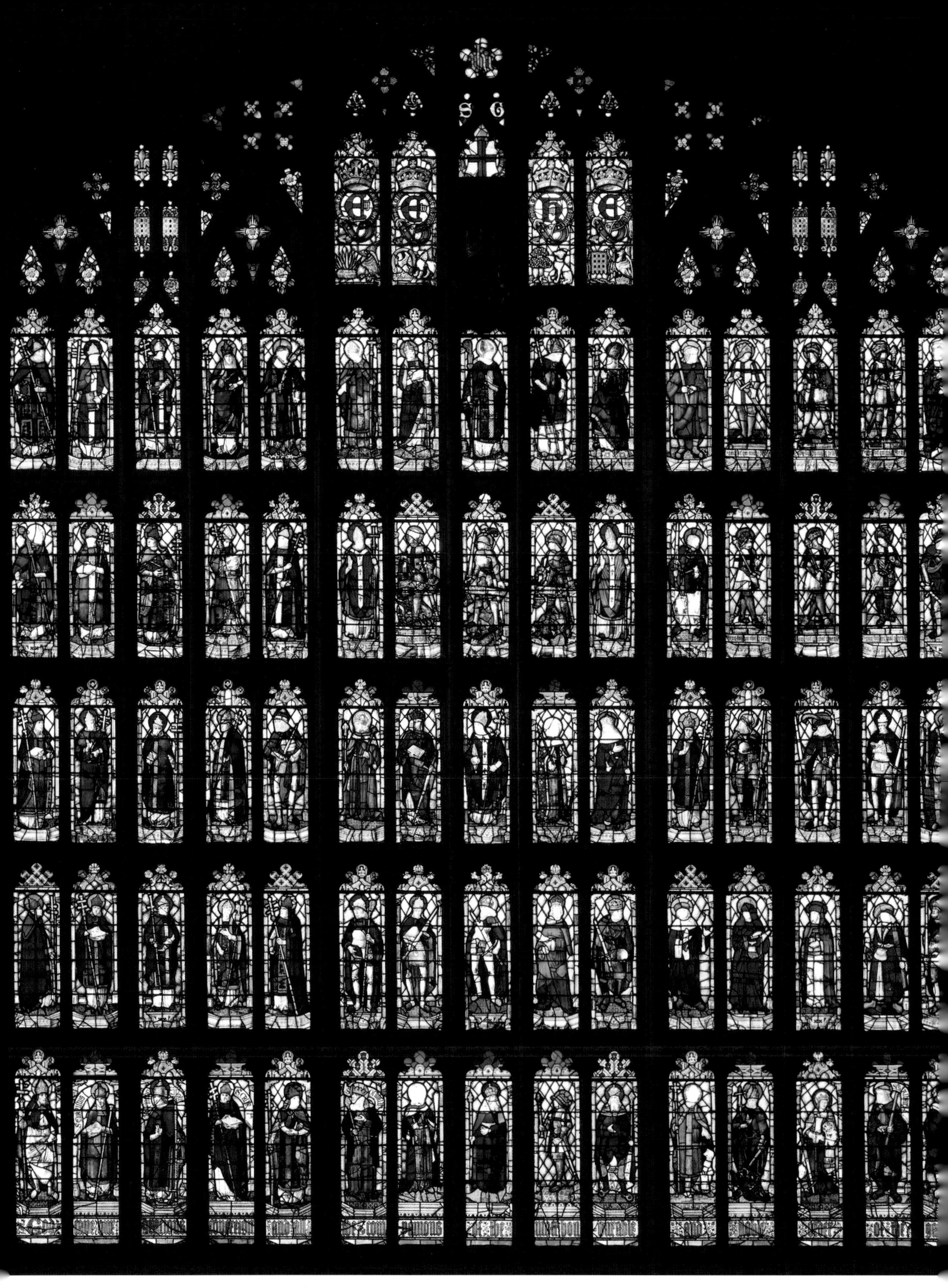

Fig 4.14 The West Window of St George's Chapel, completed c.1506

Fig 4.15 Crossing vaulting incorporating the coats of arms of Henry VIII and his Knights of the Garter, 1528

The magnificent West Window (Fig 4.14), which was inserted in the reign of Henry VII, remains the third largest stained-glass window in Great Britain. Whilst the identities of the glaziers entrusted with the project remain unknown, it is likely that much of the work was assigned to the workshop of the King's Glazier, Barnard Flower, who was subsequently commissioned to glaze the windows of King's College Chapel, Cambridge. Its completion was financed from Sir Reginald Bray's bequest. With seventy-five principal lights inserted in five rows of fifteen, the window is a fine example of early Tudor craftsmanship, featuring Kings, Popes, Saints, Knights, Archbishops and Bishops, together with portraits of a doctor and a stonemason, the latter believed to represent William Vertue. Although the figures have been rearranged and reset over the centuries, in particular during major restorations in the 1840s and 1920s, the magnificent effect produced by the light shining through the West Window remains of one of the Chapel's chief treasures.

It was not until 1528 that the Chapel commenced by Edward IV in 1475 was finished with the insertion of the fine vaulting over the Crossing financed by Henry

VIII's Garter Knights: the vaulting bears their coats of arms to commemorate their sponsorship (Fig 4.15). The King abandoned his original plan of building a lantern bell-tower, presumably because of spiralling costs. The Chapel's bells therefore continued to be housed in the Curfew Tower, where they remain today. He also had to be content with the wooden organ-loft rather than the grand stone-carved *pulpitum* (a galleried screen) which he had planned. The stone purchased for it was subsequently incorporated into a fountain in the Upper Ward. Apart from a few alterations and additions, most significantly the Coade stone organ-loft, additional Garter stalls and the Victorian stained glass, the interior we see today is to all intents and purposes the one completed in 1528. With its fan- and palm-vaulting and its pendant roof-bosses, it is a magnificent example of the perpendicular style, the most technically sophisticated of British Gothic architecture.

Fig 4.16 The Quire looking west during Evensong. The ceiling, with its fan vaulting and pendant bosses, is a magnificent example of the perpendicular style

CHAPTER FIVE

Change
The Reformation, the Burial of Henry VIII and the Later Tudors

With the building work complete, the Dean and Canons of Windsor might have anticipated a quieter, more ordered life in the Chapel. It was not to be. In 1534 Dean Richard Sampson called members of the College together to announce that the Pope was no longer to be regarded as Head of the Anglican Church, the King having assumed that role under the recent Act of Supremacy of 1534. According to John Foxe, in his famous Book of Martyrs, 'the Canons hearing this were all stricken in a dump'.[5] They were right to be so, since Henry VIII's split from Rome was to herald more than a century of political upheaval and religious change.

Henry VIII's establishment of an Anglican Church independent of the Papacy was not immediately followed by liturgical change. Vestments and ornaments remained in use and, even after the introduction of biblical readings

Fig 5.1 The burning of the 'Windsor Martyrs' in 1543, engraving published in John Foxe's *Acts and Monuments*. In the centre of the lower row, Canon London is shown riding facing the tail of his horse

Fig 5.2 Henry VIII at prayer, illustration from the Black Book of the Garter, c.1534

in English from the Great Bible, which had been approved by Henry VIII in 1539, services continued to be conducted almost entirely in Latin.

Henry's religious conservatism made him treat those holding radical religious views as heretics. In 1543 two members of the College with Protestant leanings – Organist John Marbeck and Lay Clerk Robert Testwood – were convicted of heresy and were condemned to death. Although Marbeck escaped his sentence, presumably because of his influential friends, Testwood was burnt beneath the north wall of Windsor Castle, alongside Henry Filmer, a Windsor tailor, and Anthony Pierson, a radical preacher. The three men became known as the 'Windsor Martyrs' (Fig 5.1).

On the commission responsible for their trial were Dean William Franklyn, and Canon John London. London played a key role in persecuting religious radicals nationally on behalf of Bishop Gardiner. However, Henry VIII backed Archbishop Cranmer in his struggle for power against Gardiner and Canon London was convicted of perjury. As punishment, London was forced to ride through Windsor, Reading, and Newbury facing the tail of his horse before being sent to the Fleet Prison in London, where he died in 1543.

Henry VIII's religious conservatism was further witnessed by his will, in which he expressed his wish for the establishment of a chantry at St George's Chapel, Windsor, for himself and his favourite wife, Queen Jane Seymour. His chantry chapel was to include

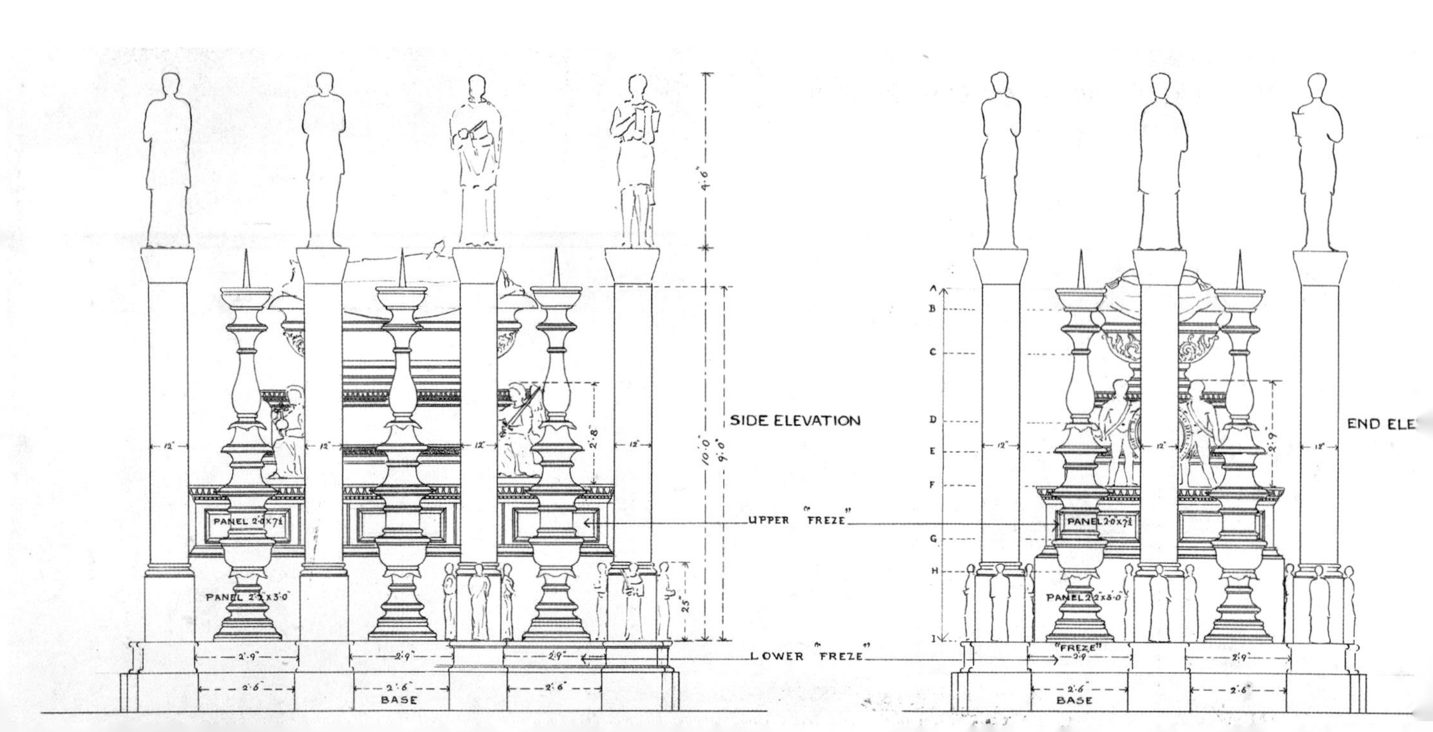

Fig 5.4 Sketch by AY Nutt of the vault below the Quire when it was opened in 1888. The coffins of Jane Seymour, Henry VIII, and Charles I may be seen from right to left

an altar where masses were to be said for their souls by two priests appointed for that purpose, and a vast commemorative tomb for the dignified burial of their bodies. The grand memorial monument was to incorporate a sarcophagus sculpted by Benedetto da Rovezzano in his studio in Westminster (Fig 5.3). Originally commissioned by Cardinal Wolsey for his own tomb, it had been confiscated by the King, along with other elements intended for Wolsey's tomb, on the Cardinal's fall from grace in 1529.

After an impressive funeral at Windsor in 1547, Henry VIII's coffin was placed beside Jane Seymour's in a modest brick vault in the centre of the Quire intended as a temporary resting-place. However, the tomb monument was not completed in his life-time and, despite further work on it commissioned by Edward VI and Elizabeth I and its transfer from Westminster to Windsor in 1567, Henry VIII and Queen Jane were never interred within it and remain buried under the Quire.

Henry VIII's will further specified the bequest of lands and other properties to the Dean and Canons to endow his chantry and to establish the Poor Knights of Windsor on a firm financial footing. He was aware that the Poor Knights, who had formed part of the College since 1348, had not been properly provided for by their founder. Numbering only one, two or three at any one time, instead of the twenty-six envisaged by Edward III, their housing and maintenance arrangements were clearly inadequate. Henry VIII's intention that their establishment should be fixed at thirteen and that they should be provided with decent alms-houses and adequate stipends, paid for by the income from the bequeathed properties, was honoured by his children.

Fig 5.5 The Poor (now Military) Knights' lodgings looking east towards the Round Tower

◀ Fig 5.3 Conjectural reconstruction of Henry VIII's tomb drawn for Alfred Higgins' paper 'On the work of Florentine sculptors in England in the early part of the sixteenth century', 1894

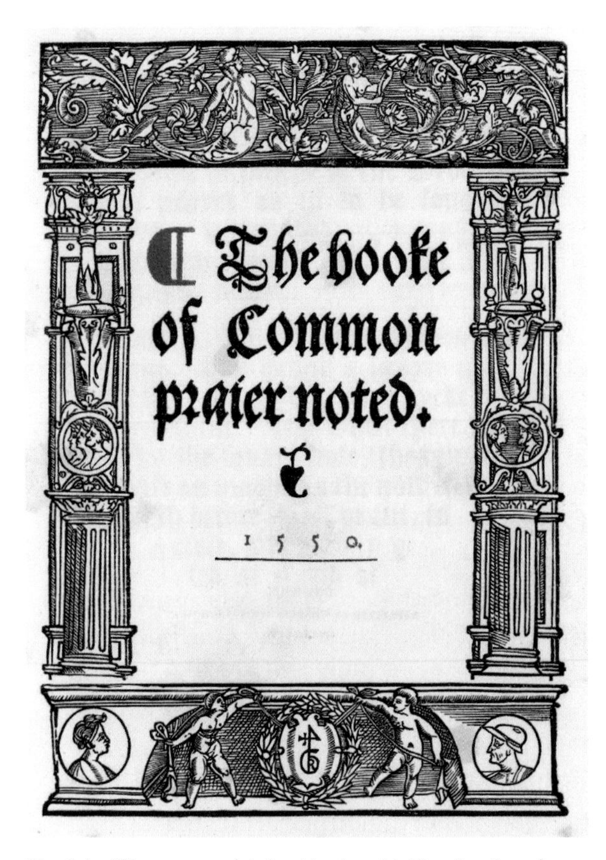

The booke of Common praier noted.

1550.

Fig 5.6 Title page of John Marbeck's *The Booke of Common Praier Noted*, 1550

Edward VI (1547–1553) arranged for the transfer of royal lands and other properties, intended to produce a net annual income of £600, to the Dean and Canons of Windsor. Mary I (1553–1558) arranged for the refurbishment of a number of houses in Lower Ward and the construction of new ones to accommodate the army veterans, and began to draw up Statutes for the regulation of the re-founded establishment. A specified part of the income from the donated properties, which were collectively known as 'the lands of the New Dotation', was used to finance the maintenance of thirteen almsmen, who were obliged to pray daily in the Chapel for the Sovereign and the Knights of the Garter, past and present. The new Statutes drafted in the reign of Mary I were ratified and issued in 1559 by her younger sister, Elizabeth I (1558–1603). The rejuvenated establishment would be better organised, more financially secure, and hold a more prestigious status from that time onwards.

The religious reforms brought in by Edward VI's government at the start of his reign in 1547 included significant changes to worship and the abandonment of vestments, ornamentation and relics. A reduction in services was to be matched by an increase in preaching. The Dean and Canons were to deliver a sermon every Sunday, whilst Edward IV's Chantry Priests, renamed 'King Edward's Preachers', were to travel outside Windsor Castle to preach for thirteen weeks a year.

In 1549, an Act of Uniformity introduced the compulsory use of the first English Book of Common Prayer, which had been drafted at Windsor where its chief author, Dr Richard Cox, was Canon from 1548 to 1553. It was subsequently set to music by another member of the College, John Marbeck, the Organist who had narrowly escaped burning for heresy

Fig 5.7 Portraits of Philip II and Mary I from the Blue Book of the Garter, 1554

in the reign of Henry VIII. His musical setting of the liturgy, entitled *The Book of Common Prayer Noted*, was published in 1550 and is still in regular use in St George's Chapel (Fig 5.6).

The second Book of Common Prayer, issued in 1552, introduced further changes. For example, the use of church-plate was restricted and the word 'table' was used instead of 'altar' to emphasise the communal nature of the Eucharist. In 1552 Commissioners visited St George's Chapel and confiscated items of church-plate and jewels, leaving the Dean and Canons with only a few vestments, chalices and patens. However, the Chapel was granted exemption from the Chantry Acts of 1545 and 1547 and was able to maintain its chantries, and the property associated with them.

Mary I's reign (1553–1558) restored Roman Catholicism, and the Chapel was dutifully restocked with missals, antiphoners, vestments, altar cloths, crosses and other items used in Roman Catholic worship. Five Protestant Canons were ejected, including reformers Richard Cox and Richard Turner, whilst several other Canons resigned, along with the Dean, William Franklyn. They were replaced in 1554 by a new Dean, Owen Oglethorpe, and nine new Canons. Embracing the traditional aspects of the Order of the Garter, Mary I revoked the Statutes introduced by Edward VI, reverting to those of Henry VIII. She also reinstated former Garter Knight Thomas Howard, 3rd Duke of Norfolk (degraded by Edward VI in 1547) and installed her husband, Philip II of Spain, into the Order shortly after his arrival in England in 1554. Philip II celebrated several Garter Feasts and installations at Windsor during his short sojourns in England.

A change of monarch in 1558 brought further alterations to Chapel worship and to the Garter ceremony. Elizabeth I (1558–1603) reverted to the Edwardian Anglican settlement, reinstating the Book of Common Prayer and ordering the abandonment

Fig 5.8 Garter stall-plate of Thomas Howard, 4th Duke of Norfolk, degraded for treason, now in the South Quire Aisle

of Roman Catholic practices. Not all the members of the Windsor Chapter were willing to embrace the return to Protestantism: Dean Boxall resigned his office in 1560 and two of the most committed Roman Catholic Canons, William Chedsey and Thomas Slythurst, were deprived of their canonries and imprisoned in London in 1559.

However, religious conservative, Canon Richard Bruerne, who was accused by his fellow Canons of being a 'manifest papist, a maintainer of superstition [such] as altars crosses and candles'[6] retained his Canonry until his death in 1565. Meanwhile, the now redundant ornaments, vestments and jewels were distributed for sale among the Dean and Canons. Visiting Windsor in 1570, Sir Nicholas Bacon was appalled by this behaviour and ordered the return of any unsold items with any profits from sales going to the College's Aerary (Treasury).

Elizabeth I reasserted the ceremony and tradition of the Order of the Garter. She transformed the Garter festivities, which were increasingly held at Whitehall or Greenwich rather than Windsor, into great public spectacles during which the Queen, arrayed in Garter robes and a diadem of pearls upon her head, processed under a hand-held canopy preceded by her Knights and Heralds 'in the manner of that solemn and triumphant proceeding'.[7] However, by transferring the Garter Feasts and other ceremonies from Windsor, a practice which was formalised by an ordinance of 1567, the importance of St George's Chapel as a Royal Free Chapel was on the wane. The installations of Garter Knights at Windsor were undertaken by proxies on her behalf; whilst the Deans and Canons appointed by Elizabeth I were not the influential courtiers and eminent religious scholars favoured by her father, Henry VIII, and brother, Edward VI.

Meanwhile building works undertaken on Windsor Castle during Elizabeth's reign were largely confined to the Upper Ward. The Queen's Private Chapel, which formed part of the State Apartments, underwent a major reconstruction and refurbishment in the 1570s, with a new painted ceiling installed and new choir-stalls and panelling introduced. The works cost of nearly £2,000. When Elizabeth I visited Windsor, this was the Royal Chapel she attended.

Fig 5.9 Elizabeth I taking part in a Garter procession, conjectural engraving by Wenceslaus Hollar for Elias Ashmole's *The Institutions, Laws and Ceremonies of the Most Noble Order of the Garter* (1672)

CHAPTER SIX

Beautification
The Early Stuarts

The first two Stuart Kings, James I (1603–1625) and Charles I (1625–1649), who appointed distinguished theologians to the Windsor Chapter, encouraged the beautification of worship in the Chapel and took the leading part in Garter services and processions at Windsor. The notable Deans who served at this time included Giles Tomson (Dean 1603–1612), who was appointed as one of the translators of the King James Bible, Marco Antonio de Dominis (Dean 1618–1622), a Roman Catholic bishop and intellectual who defected to Britain in 1616 having fallen out with the Pope over payments due to the Papal See, and brothers Matthew and Christopher Wren (Deans 1627–1635 and 1635–1659), who introduced more elaborate ritual and ceremonial into the services following the example of Archbishop Laud.

Fig 6.1 Memorial in the Bray Chantry Chapel to Bishop Giles Tomson, Dean 1603-12, one of the translators of the King James Bible

Matthew Wren, uncle and patron of the famous architect Sir Christopher Wren, was an influential figure within the Church of England and at Charles I's Royal Court. As Dean of Windsor, he worked closely with the King to replace the Chapel's plate surrendered at the time of the Reformation. After a lengthy fund-raising campaign, involving several appeals to the Knights of the Garter and a personal donation of £100 from the King,

Fig 6.2 Matthew Wren, Dean 1627–1635, engraving by Gerard Vandergucht, 1750

sufficient cash was raised to commission the new plate from Christiaen van Vianen, the leading London-based goldsmith and silversmith of the day. The Utrecht-born master craftsman produced a spectacular series of silver plate decorated with scenes from the Bible. Dean Matthew Wren was also active in his role as Register of the Order of the Garter and devoted much time to reviewing and clarifying the Garter Statutes. His brother and successor as Dean, Christopher Wren, continued his efforts and introduced proposals for the renovation of the Order in 1637, including the reintroduction of the traditional blue mantles (cloaks) worn by the Garter Knights.

In the same year, 1637, the Dean and Canons commissioned a new organ by Emmanuel Cresswell of Wolverhampton at a cost of £110. It was lavishly praised by the King:

> Soe you have offered an instrument of praise to fill upp the melody of voyces w[hi]ch praise the Lord ... So that there rests noe more on your part but ... to pray for the King and all his noble knights in this Quire that they may make up a part of the Quire in Heaven, w[hi]ch you have modelized in your Chappell.[8]

Charles I took a keen personal interest in the Order of the Garter. Even after he lost possession in the English Civil War of the two traditional venues for Garter events, Windsor Castle and Whitehall Palace, the King convened a further Garter Feast in York in 1642, and he continued to appoint new Knights Companions after he had been imprisoned. Charles I was to return to Windsor Castle, in 1647 and 1648, but this time as a prisoner. His final journey to Windsor, in 1649, was in a coffin.

Fig 6.3 Deanery oak table

Fig 6.4 Portrait of Charles I from the Red Book of the Garter

After Charles I had been beheaded at Whitehall, on 30 January 1649, following a trial at Westminster Hall, Sir Thomas Herbert, former Groom of the Bedchamber, begged permission to bury the King in Westminster Abbey. This request was denied by Parliament. However, Herbert was permitted to arrange the King's burial at St George's Chapel. On 7 February, the embalmed body was brought from St James' Palace to Windsor on a black velvet-covered hearse and was taken to the Deanery, where it may have been placed on the Jacobean table currently in the Dean's study (Fig 6.3). It is sometimes alleged that the King's head was sewn back onto his body on this table, but there is no evidence to corroborate this. The coffin was then transported to the State Apartments where it lay overnight, before its final journey to St George's Chapel the following morning. Carried 'by gentlemen of quality in mourning'[9] the coffin was lowered into the small vault in the centre of the Quire, where it was placed beside the body of Henry VIII. The Bishop of London, Bishop Juxon, who was present with the Governor of Windsor Castle and a small number of nobles and gentlemen, stood ready with a service book to officiate at the burial. However, the Governor forbade the use of the Book of Common Prayer, and so, according

Fig 6.4 Ledger stone recording the burial of Jane Seymour, Henry VIII, Charles I and an infant child of Queen Anne in a vault beneath the Quire

to Lord Clarendon, 'the King's body was laid, without any words, or other ceremonies than the tears and sighs of a few beholders'.[10]

The burial vault remained unmarked for almost two hundred years until, in 1837, William IV had a ledger-stone inserted in the Quire pavement to mark the spot. The black ledger-stone, inscribed with the names Henry VIII, Jane Seymour, and Charles I, was in fact incorrectly located to the west of their actual burial place, which is nearer the High Altar. The year of Charles I's death is recorded as 1648 (rather than 1649), following the 'old style' dating system.

CHAPTER SEVEN

Conflict
The English Civil War (1642–1651) and its Aftermath (1652–1660)

In October 1642, Colonel John Venn and twelve companies of foot soldiers took possession of Windsor Castle on behalf of Parliament without a shot fired. With Parliamentary troops occupying the Castle, it was merely a question of time before Governor Venn would seek to have the Dean and Canons ejected from the Lower Ward. The House of Lords attempted to preserve the College of St George from harm, ordering the Speaker to write to Colonel Venn 'to take care that there be no disorders and disturbances made in the Chapel at Windsor; and that the evidences, registers, monuments there and all things that belong to the Order of the Garter, may be preserved without any defacings; and that he permit the Prebends [Canons] to live in their own houses'.[11] However, the House of Commons passed an ordinance expelling them from Windsor Castle and, on 23 May 1643, the Dean and Canons, bowing to the inevitable, petitioned the Lords that 'they may

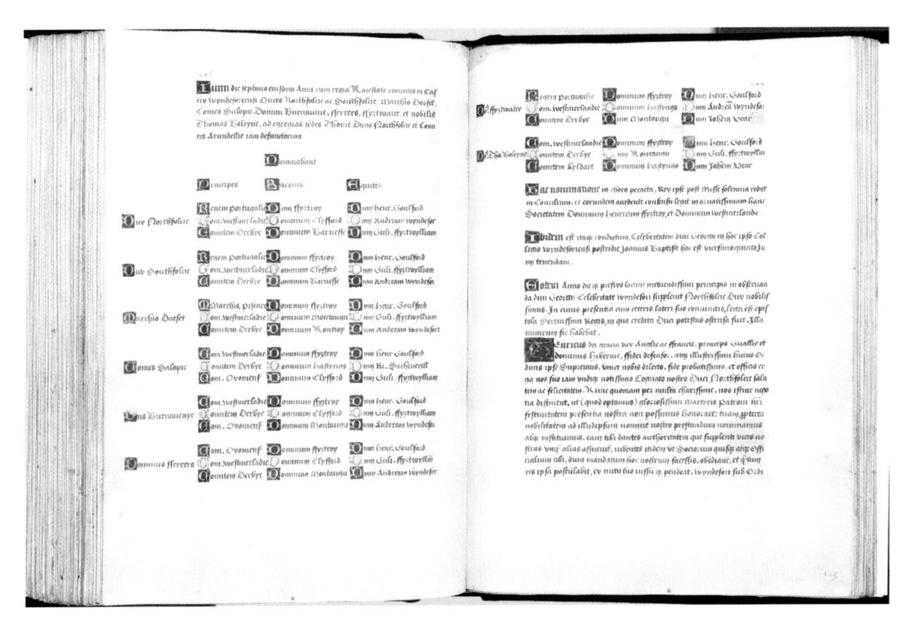

Fig 7.1 Illuminated pages from the Black Book of the Garter

Fig 7.2 Portrait of Christopher Wren, Dean and Register of the Order of the Garter 1635–1659, holding the Red Book of the Garter

Fig 7.3 Giant candlestick copied from an original made for Henry VIII's tomb, sold by the Parliamentarians in the 17th century and now in St Bavo's Cathedral, Ghent. The replica cast in 1929 for St George's Chapel as a commemorative gift from the King and Queen, stands near the High Altar

have liberty to carry forth all their goods, utensils, household stuffs and books to their several abodes, and that an order might be made for their safe conveying and quiet enjoying of the same'.[12] Dean Christopher Wren, prior to his departure to the parish of East Knoyle in Wiltshire, managed to recover and preserve three registers of the Order of the Garter (the Black, Blue and Red Books): these are now held in the Chapel archives (Fig 7.1).

With the Dean and Canons of Windsor gone, the Parliamentarians surveyed and confiscated their vast estates, selling many of them to the College's former tenants. At Windsor, Colonel Venn acquired the Deanery for his own use and turned his

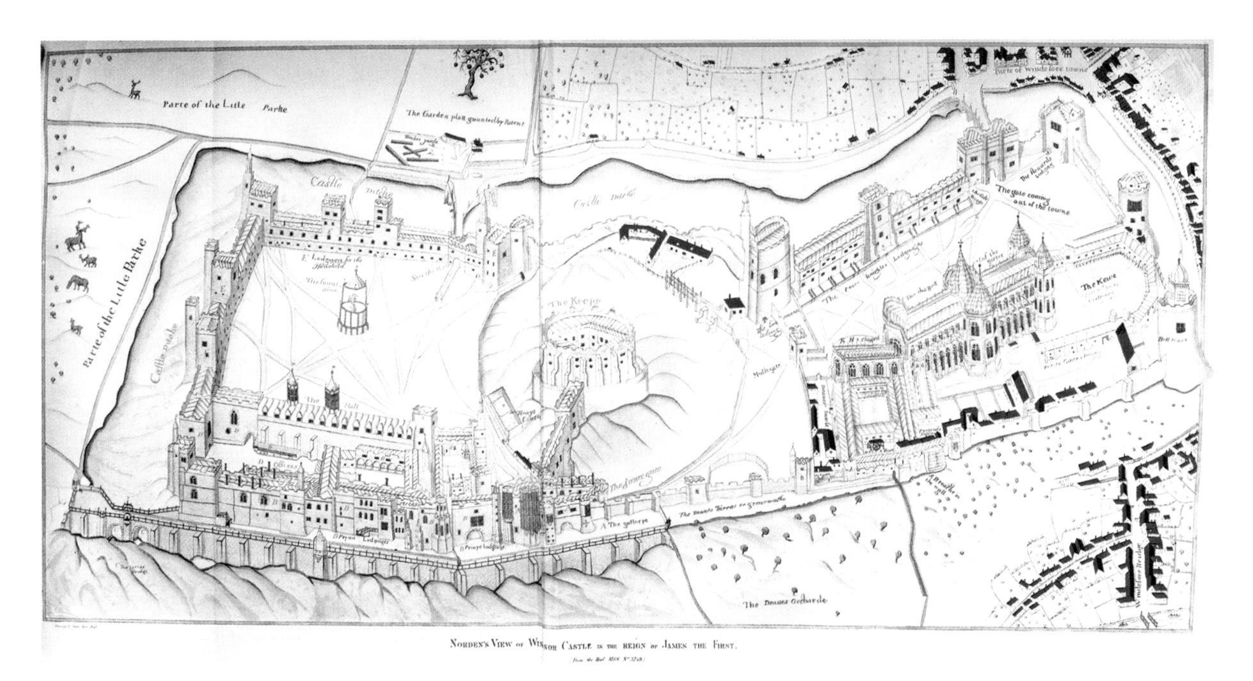

Fig 7.4 John Norden's bird's-eye view of Windsor Castle painted in 1607, reproduced in R R Tighe and J E Davis, *Annals of Windsor* (1858) from an original in the British Library (Harleian MS 3749, f.3)

Fig 7.5 The Lower Ward of Windsor Castle looking west, with Crane's Building in the centre, copied from a 17th century drawing by Wenceslas Hollar

attention to the contents of the Chapel. The coat of mail belonging to Edward IV, with its surcoat of crimson velvet decorated with pearls and rubies, was seized from above his tomb, and many other treasures were removed and sold, including the brass statues and candlesticks intended for Henry VIII's tomb (Fig 7.3).

The Chapel's plate was melted down and coined to finance Sir Thomas Fairfax's northern campaign. But all was not lost. The fabric of the Chapel, including the stained-glass windows, stone carvings, mediaeval woodwork and Garter stall-plates, survived intact and the Chapel continued to be used for the delivery of sermons to the inhabitants of Windsor Castle, albeit of a very different nature from before. New and recast bells were added to the Curfew Tower in 1650, two of which are still in use today. John Evelyn, during a visit to St George's Chapel with his wife, made no mention of any noticeable damage to the Chapel fabric in his diary entry for 8 June 1654:

> We din'd at Windsor, saw the Castle and Chapell of St. George, where they have laied our blessed Martyr, King Charles in the vault just before ye alter. The church and workmanship in stone is admirable.[13]

Meanwhile the Poor Knights of Windsor, an integral part of the College of St George since its foundation in 1348, were allowed to remain in residence in the Castle, supported by income from some of the confiscated College estates. With Oliver Cromwell's approval, their number was increased from thirteen to eighteen, under the terms of the will of Sir Francis Crane. A block of almshouses, known as Crane's Building, was constructed to accommodate the additional veterans. It stood against the west wall of the Castle until its demolition in 1847 (Fig 7.5). The Poor Knights were present at Cromwell's funeral at Westminster Abbey in November 1658. During the Parliamentary occupation of the Castle, they kept the spirit of the College alive and were there to greet the Dean and Canons on their return on the Restoration of the Monarchy in 1660.

▸ Fig 7.6 Two Poor Knights of Windsor, one of a series of drawings by Peter Lely, 1663–1671, in the British Museum

Fig 8.1 Bruno Ryves, Dean 1660–77, portrait by an unknown artist

CHAPTER EIGHT

Restoration
The Later Stuarts

St George's Chapel was one of the first religious establishments to be reconstituted by Charles II (1660–1685) on his accession to the throne in May 1660. Five of the twelve Canons ejected in 1643 returned to Windsor Castle, in company with five Minor Canons and the Organist, William Child. The remaining vacancies were soon filled, although not all by Royalists and High-Churchmen: Canon George Evans, for example, had served as a Presbyterian minister in the Commonwealth.

By July 1660 there was a full complement of Canons and the new Dean, Bruno Ryves,

Fig 8.2 St George's House looking east. The building was constructed in the seond half of the 17th century

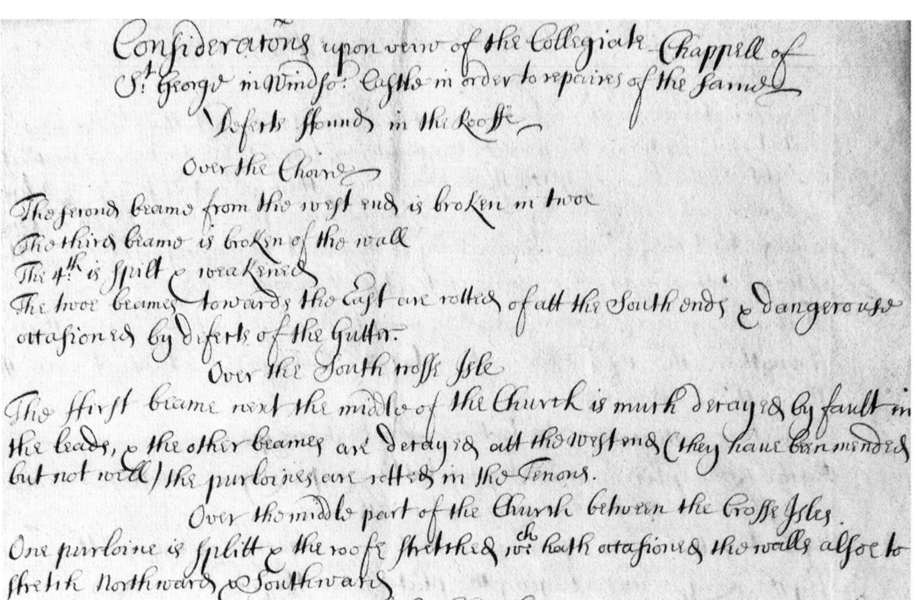
Considerations upon view of the Collegiate Chappell of
St George in Windsor Castle in order to repaires of the same
Defects founds in the Roofe
Over the Choire
The second beame from the west end is broken in two
The third beame is broken of the wall
The 4th is split & weakned
The two beames towards the East are rotted of all the South ends & dangerous
occasioned by defects of the Gutter.
Over the South crosse Isle
The first beame next the middle of the Church is much decayed by fault in
the leads, & the other beames are decayed all the west end (they have been mended
but not well) the purloines are rotted in the Tenons.
Over the middle part of the Church between the Crosse Isles.
One purloine is split & the roofe stretched, wch hath occasioned the walls alsoe to
stretch Northward & Southward

Fig 8.3 Condition survey by Sir Christopher Wren, 1682

was appointed in August in place of Dean Christopher Wren, who had died in 1659. He was installed in the Chapel on 3 September 1660.

On the return of the Dean and Canons there was much to do. Most of the Canons' houses had to be restored or totally rebuilt. The building now occupied by St George's House, dates from this period. It replaced the fourteenth-century houses on the west side of the Canons' Cloister, which were presumably deemed beyond repair. The Windsor Chapter concentrated its limited resources on returning these domestic buildings to a habitable state before turning its attention to the Chapel.

In 1682 the Dean and Canons consulted Sir Christopher Wren for advice on the Chapel, a building which Wren knew well because his uncle, Matthew, and father, Christopher, had served successively as Dean. His meticulous structural survey detailed the extent of the damage and decay, and included an estimate for repairs, totalling £1,012, which he advised could be spread over seven years. Work began immediately, and the replacement beams and rafters saved the roof from imminent collapse. On Wren's advice, the Dean and Canons removed the decayed heraldic statues ('King's Beasts') from the outside of the Chapel. However, they did not replace them with carved stone pineapples, as Wren had suggested, or with other sculptures despite their decorative and structural benefits.

Sir Christopher Wren was also employed by Charles II to design a grand mausoleum and monument to his father, Charles I, at the east end of St George's, on the site now occupied by the Albert Chapel. Wren's plans for a classical edifice with a domed roof, which would have involved the demolition of the existing building, were subsequently abandoned in favour of repairing and adapting it. Court artist Antonio Verrio was engaged to paint and decorate the walls and ceiling under the terms of a contract worth £1,000. The mausoleum was never completed, and the Chapel, which remained the responsibility of the Crown rather than the Dean and Canons, once more fell into disuse.

Within St George's Chapel itself services resumed, with the additional pomp and ceremony advocated by Archbishop Laud. The newly-appointed Presbyterian Canon, George Evans, found this difficult to accept.

He refused, for example, to bow to the altar, even at the Garter Service in 1661, at which the King was present and observed 'If he will not bow to God, let him not bow to me'.[14] Shortly afterwards Canon Evans renounced Presbyterianism and was ordained into the Church of England.

Meanwhile Charles II revelled in the ceremony and pageantry of the Order of the Garter and led the Knights Companions by example in donating money towards expensive new plate for the Chapel. The new plate included 'a pair of wrought Flaggons, with great bellies, having the Figure of St George on Horseback on the Covers, the rest all Feather-work, bought with the Knights money, weighing 414 Ounces',[15] basins, chalices, covers and candlesticks, which are still in use on ceremonial occasions in the Chapel today. Furnishings and ornaments were also purchased and a new organ was commissioned from Robert Dallam, who was 'to have 600£ for it', to replace the instrument made by his father, Thomas Dallam, which had been removed in the Commonwealth.[16]

St George's Chapel had resumed much of its pomp and prestige, but the battle to recover the properties from which the College formerly drew its income continued for a long time. These lands, rectories and other possessions had been appropriated by the Parliamentarians during the Civil War and, although some had been retained in trust for the maintenance of the Poor Knights, many had been sold. Since this was a problem shared across the Church of England, the King established a Royal Commission to enquire into the 'pretended sale and purchases' of Church lands, and to supervise their recovery as peacefully as possible. The original owners were obliged to pay compensation to the purchasers, which in the case of the Windsor Chapter amounted to approximately £9,000, or to initiate law-suits to reclaim property withheld from them, the Dean and Canons incurring legal costs of at least £510. A further £6,100 was paid out to supplement the incomes of vicarages and curacies for which they resumed responsibility. It had been a lengthy and expensive business but, by the end of the seventeenth century, the College had restored its income as well as its status as a leading property owner.

Fig 8.4 Feathered flagon, one of pair commissioned by Charles II c.1662

James II (1685–1688), who came to the throne on the death of his brother in 1685, continued to pay Antonio Verrio for the decoration of the Lady Chapel commenced by Charles II, although there is no evidence that he used it for Roman Catholic worship as is sometimes claimed. During his reign, the Quire of St George's Chapel was paved with the black and white marble squares which are still in use today. The paving was paid for by Organist William Child in somewhat unusual circumstances.

During the reign of Charles II, William Child had been owed nearly £500 in salary by the King. Believing that this amount was unlikely to be paid, the Organist agreed to sell his right to repayment (presumably in the form of a credit note) to the Canons for £5 and some bottles of wine, and signed a bond transferring the debt to them. On his accession to the throne, James II unexpectedly agreed to pay off arrears that had arisen under his brother, Charles II, and Child was filled with regret that he had missed out. The Canons generously agreed to release him from his agreement, enabling Child to receive the repayment, on condition that he financed the paving of the Quire. Child did so and this fact is recorded on his grave-stone in the North Quire Aisle.

Fig 8.5 Black and white photograph of the Quire paving, paid for by Organist William Child in about 1685. The ledger stone inserted in 1837 is in the foreground

James II was driven out of England on account of his overt Roman Catholicism in the so-called 'Glorious Revolution' of 1688, and was succeeded by his elder daughter, Mary, who assumed the throne with her husband, William of Orange, Stadtholder of the Netherlands. Shortly after their arrival in England, Prince William and Princess Mary visited Windsor Castle and met the Dean, Dr Hascard. On 11 April 1689, they were crowned as William III (1689–1702) and Mary II (1689–1694), ensuring the Protestantism of the future monarchy and ushering in a period of relative peace and prosperity.

Not all the members of Chapter were in favour of the new regime. Dr John Fitzwilliams had been Chaplain to James as Duke of York, and Tutor to his daughter, Princess Anne, and was the only Canon of Windsor to have been appointed by James II. His loyalty to the deposed King prevented him from taking the oath of allegiance to William and Mary required of all the Anglican clergy and, although he continued to reside from time to time in Windsor until 1691, he was in that year deprived of his Canonry.

Apart from the loss of one of their Canons, the College of St George continued its worship in a relatively peaceful way and there is little to report during the reign of the final Stuart monarch, Queen Anne (1702–1714), who acceded to the throne on 8 March 1702 on the death of her brother-in-law, William III. She was very fond of Windsor Castle and spent

Fig 8.6 Gregory Hascard, Dean 1684–1708, portrait by an unknown artist

much time there, residing in the Queen's Lodge opposite the South Terrace. Other than renovating the Lodge she was not inclined to undertake significant building works either in the Upper Ward of the Castle or in St George's Chapel. One of her many stillborn children is buried in the vault under the Quire.

Queen Anne took a great interest in the Order of the Garter, appointing fourteen Knights Companions during her twelve-year reign. The first two of these, Wriothesley Russell, Duke of Bedford, and John Churchill, later Duke of Marlborough, were invested on 14 March 1702, shortly after the Queen's accession. On this occasion, Queen Anne was advised that female sovereigns should wear the Garter on their left arm above the elbow, a custom adopted by all Queens and Ladies Companions ever since.

Meanwhile the Dean and Canons carried out minor repairs on the Chapel and domestic buildings in their care and continued to hold daily services. It was not a time of significant change at St George's Chapel either in terms of architecture or religious worship.

Fig 8.7 Queen Anne and the Knights of the Garter, painting by Peter Angelis c.1725

CHAPTER NINE

Revival
The House of Hanover

The low profile of the Chapel continued under the first two monarchs of the House of Hanover, George I (1714–1727) and George II (1727–1760), who showed very little interest in Windsor. Indeed this period in the history of Windsor Castle has been described as 'the Big Sleep'. This was to change with the accession of George III (1760–1820).

At the beginning of his reign, George III made only brief visits to Windsor principally to enjoy the hunting in the Great Park, lodging his growing family in the Queen's Lodge and nearby Burford House, which he purchased and renamed Lower Lodge. Gradually the stays became longer and more frequent and in 1776 the King seems to have come to a decision to make Windsor his preferred residence. In August of that year George III and his family first worshipped in St George's Chapel. Having walked from the Queen's Lodge to the south door, they were welcomed by the Dean and Canons and the Poor Knights. Members of the Royal Family were to become regular worshippers in St George's, either occupying stalls in the Quire or observing the services from the Royal Closet, the oriel window added to the Edward IV Chantry Chapel for

Fig 9.1 The interior of the Edward IV Chantry Chapel, featuring the decorated woodwork added by Henry Emlyn in the 18th century, when it became known as the Royal Closet

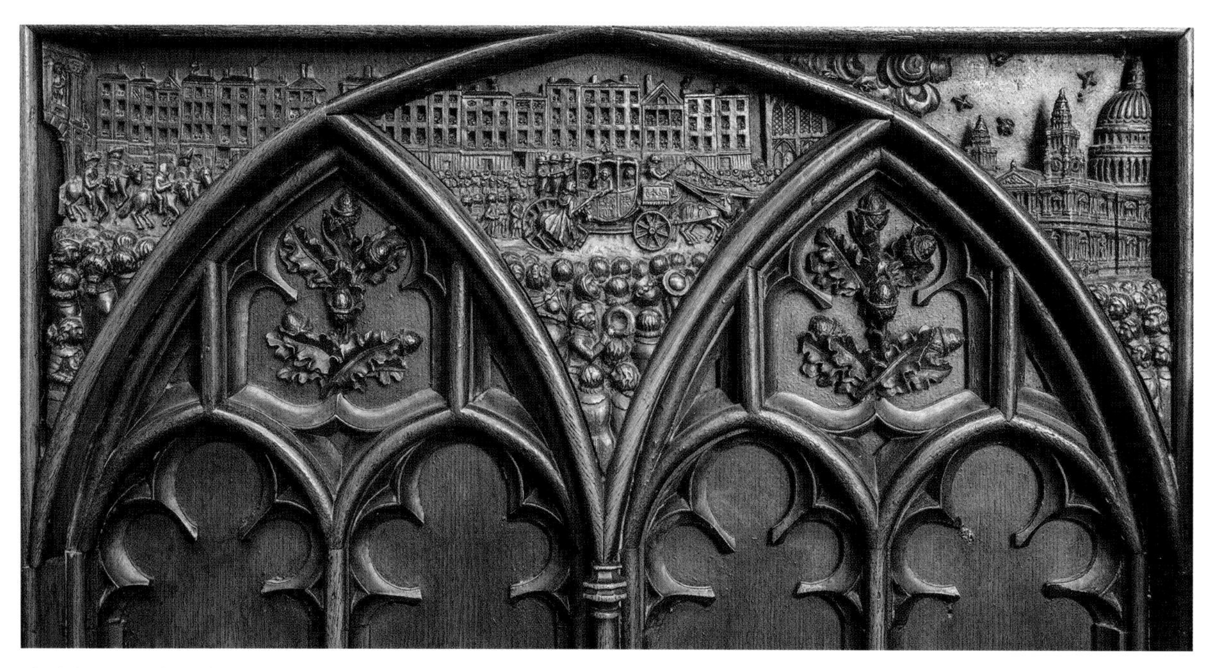

Fig 9.2 Desk front in the Quire by Henry Emlyn, showing George III riding in a carriage at Westminster, 18th century

Katherine of Aragon. In 1785 the Royal Closet was refurbished and a fine new staircase was added to allow easier access via the Vestry.

This refurbishment was part of a much wider programme of building works in St George's Chapel, commissioned and largely funded by George III and the Knights of the Garter. These 'great works' included the introduction of a new organ-screen and font, both constructed out of the fashionable artificial stone known as Coade stone, the insertion of heraldic stained glass designed by Francis Eginton in the Clerestory (upper) windows of the Quire, the re-fashioning of Edward IV's tomb in the North Quire Aisle and the replacement of the East Window with a painted-glass depiction of the Resurrection of Christ, designed by Benjamin West and painted by Thomas Jervais. The High Altar was replaced, and a painting of the Last Supper, also by Benjamin West, was installed behind it. The painted vaulting in the South Quire Aisle was lime-washed and the whole Chapel was 'cleaned and decorated', as Horace Walpole observed, to create 'a scene of lightness and graces'.[17]

This major building project, which entailed the complete closure of the Chapel from 1787 to 1790 and included the relocation of a number of monuments and ledger stones, cost at least £21,000, of which £14,000 came from the King's Privy Purse and £7,000 was contributed by the Knights of the Garter and the Dean and Canons. The man responsible for overseeing these works was Canon Fisher, whilst much of the design and wood-carving was undertaken by local craftsman and aspiring architect, Henry Emlyn. Of particular note are the additional Garter stalls, two on either side of the Quire, which were carved to accommodate the increased number of Garter Knights created by George III. Replicating the form of the original fifteenth-century stalls, they were exquisitely carved with contemporary scenes to celebrate the reign of George III.

George III took a considerable interest in the Order of the Garter and was keen that all seven of his adult sons should be able to join. In order to achieve this, he arranged for the Garter Statutes to be altered to allow the appointment of additional (Supernumerary) Garter Knights, to supplement the existing number of twenty-six. These Supernumeraries were to include members of the Royal Family, in particular descendants of George I and George II, as well as overseas monarchs and princes (known as Stranger Knights) who had previously been counted within the Companionship of twenty-six. George III held many investitures for new Garter Knights during his long reign and regularly attended Garter Chapter meetings. However, the practice of holding grand Garter Feasts seems to have lapsed, and very few installations took place within St George's Chapel in the later eighteenth century. Indeed, there were none between 1772 and 1804. However, in 1805, the King spent nearly £11,000 on preparations for Garter Day, the first attempt for many years to hold the Garter Feast and other ceremonies in the manner laid down by the Garter Statutes. In 1804, George III had moved into recently-renovated apartments in the Upper Ward overlooking the North Terrace. He then set about adapting the State Apartments to prepare them for the forthcoming Garter celebrations, fitting out St George's Hall with an organ and a music-gallery, and setting up five temporary kitchens to create a splendid Garter feast.

Fig 9.3 Admission ticket for the 1805 Garter installation service

After dining, the Garter Knights and Knights-elect processed down Chapel Hill accompanied by the Poor and Naval Knights,[18] Canons, Pursuivants and Heralds, Garter Officers, Yeomen of the Guard and Royal Household Officers, to the south door of the Chapel, where the procession split. The Canons and the Poor and Naval Knights took their places in the Quire, whilst the Garter Knights and Knights-elect made their way to the Garter Chapter House, by then incorporated into the Deanery. In due course the Garter procession made its way into the Chapel, where the new Garter Knights were installed. The service which followed lasted for several hours, at the end of which the procession reformed and made its way back to the State Apartments. It had been a spectacular occasion, witnessed by the large crowds who flocked to Windsor.

However, there was a great deal of chaos both within and outside the Chapel, with overcrowding, partly due to the re-use of tickets. Many people, having been admitted to their stands in the Chapel, threw down their tickets to their friends below. Not all the spectators were impressed. Charles Knight, who was to become a notable journalist and a future Mayor of Windsor, who viewed the procession from a parapet, described it as 'a frightful spectacle of fat, limping, leaden supporters of chivalry'.[19] It was to be the last full Garter Service held at Windsor until 1911.

In 1804, the year before the Garter Service, George III had commissioned the construction of a new royal vault at Windsor underneath the chapel known as the Tomb House, which housed Henry VIII's unfinished tomb (now reconfigured as the Albert Chapel). His great-grandfather, George I, had been buried in Hanover, whilst his grandfather, George II, and his father, Frederick, Prince of Wales, had been interred in a large new royal vault beneath Westminster Abbey commissioned by George II on the death of Queen Caroline. However, George III's fondness for Windsor prompted him to fund the construction of a mausoleum there for his own family.

James Wyatt was chosen as architect and, on 3 November 1804, the Dean and Canons granted permission for 'Mr Wyatt to make an Entrance from the East End of St George's Chapel, into the Vault intended to be Erected under the Adjoining Building called the Tomb House.'[20] The brief for the Royal Vault specified that it should extend under the whole of the Tomb House, measuring almost 70 feet long by 28 feet wide. A major engineering feat, its construction necessitated the removal of the remnants of Henry VIII's tomb, the lifting of the existing floor and the excavation of the underlying chalk to a depth of almost 15 feet. The marble sarcophagus (which had originally been commissioned by Cardinal Wolsey) was transported to the crypt of St Paul's Cathedral, London, in 1808, where it was converted into a monument for national hero Admiral Horatio Nelson.

With the permission of the Dean and Canons, an entrance shaft to the new Royal Vault was constructed in the pavement of the Quire. This enabled the coffin to be lowered during the funeral service into a subterranean passage leading to the Vault, by means of a lift fitted within the shaft. Whilst excavating the shaft in 1813, workmen uncovered the unmarked vault in the centre of the Quire in which the bodies of Henry VIII, Queen Jane Seymour and Charles I were buried. After samples had been taken from the body of Charles I for testing by the King's Physician, Sir Henry Halford, the vault was closed. Apart from a brief reopening in 1888 to return

Fig 9.4 The Royal Vault in 1817, aquatint by Daniel Havell from a drawing by Frederick Nash

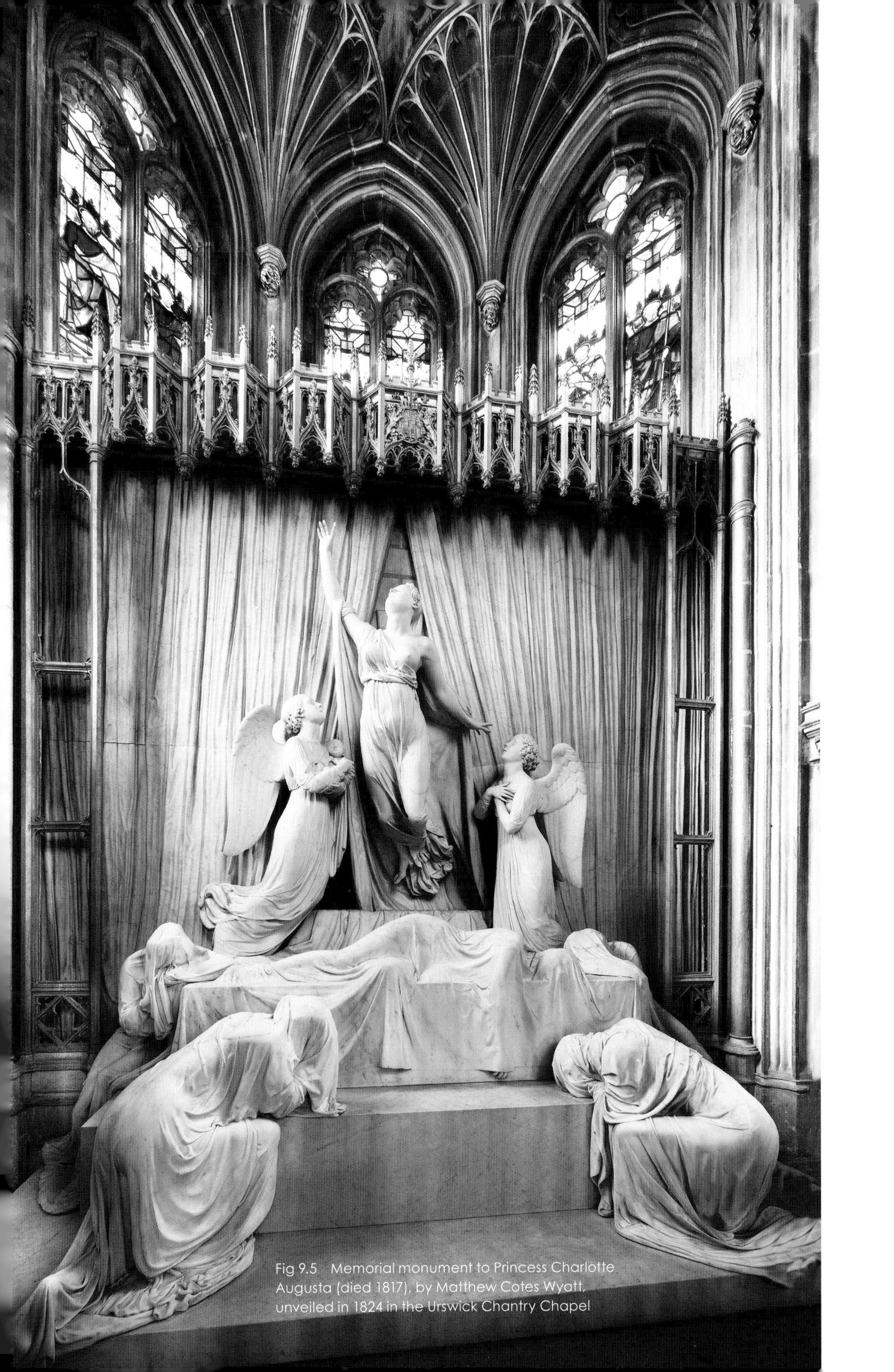

Fig 9.5 Memorial monument to Princess Charlotte Augusta (died 1817), by Matthew Cotes Wyatt, unveiled in 1824 in the Urswick Chantry Chapel

these samples, the vault has since remained undisturbed.

Meanwhile, Wyatt began to convert the former Tomb House into a Garter Chapter Room, repairing the roof, battlements and windows and installing a new plaster ceiling emblazoned with 394 shields of former Garter Knights. James Wyatt's nephew and successor, Sir Jeffry Wyatville, continued this conversion, adding a new porch in the 1830s. The porch, which was designed as a place for the Garter Knights to gather before and after Garter ceremonies, was seldom used and was demolished in 1862.

Sadly, it was not long before the Royal Vault was brought into use. In 1810, George III's beloved youngest daughter, Amelia, died at the age of twenty-seven. The shock of her death threw the King into a state of agitation and illness from which he never fully recovered. After a funeral in St George's Chapel on 13 November 1810, Princess Amelia's coffin was laid to rest in a temporary position in the unfinished Royal Vault, from which it was to be subsequently moved into one of the thirty-two niches lining the walls of the completed mausoleum. George III's sister, Augusta, Duchess of Brunswick, was to follow her into the Royal Vault after her funeral on 31 March 1813. Four years later they were joined by Princess Charlotte Augusta, who was buried there with her stillborn child in 1817. Her death, at the end of fifty hours of labour, prompted national mourning and left the succession in doubt.

Despite the fact that George III and Queen Charlotte had fifteen children, Princess Charlotte Augusta had been their only surviving legitimate grandchild. Before her death in 1817, she had been second in line to the throne after her father, George, who had been made Prince Regent in 1811 when George III was declared incapable of ruling. After 1817, the line of succession passed to her uncle, Frederick, Duke of York, and when he died childless in 1827, to his

Fig 9.6 The funeral of Princess Charlotte Augusta in St George's Chapel on 19 November 1817, engraving by T Sutherland after James Stephanoff, published in 1818

Fig 9.7 Louis Philippe, King of France, and his companions viewing Princess Charlotte Augusta's monument during a State Visit to Windsor, 1844, lithograph from a drawing by Edouard Pringet

younger brother, William, Duke of Clarence (the future William IV). Although William's wife, Princess Adelaide, gave birth to two daughters, both died in infancy. One of them, Princess Elizabeth, was buried in the Royal Vault at Windsor. It was Edward, Duke of Kent, the fourth son of George III, with his wife, Princess Victoria of Saxe-Coburg-Saalfeld, who succeeded in producing a healthy grandchild able to inherit the throne: Princess Alexandrina Victoria, who was born in 1819 and crowned as Queen Victoria in 1837.

Princess Charlotte Augusta's funeral, which was held in St George's Chapel on 19 November 1817, was a shambles. Her father, the Prince Regent (later King George IV), who was not present, had issued instructions and invitations to the funeral which were at odds with arrangements made by the Dean and Canons. Further bad feeling was caused when the Canons insisted on sitting in the stalls of the Knights of the Garter, which had been allocated to others, and many of the public could not be seated at all despite having been issued with tickets. One of these, local journalist Charles Knight, who had been invited by Chapter to report on the ceremony, was refused admittance and roughly handled by the soldiers on duty.

The chaos at the funeral did nothing to improve the poor relationship between the Prince Regent and the Dean, Henry Hobart, and resulted in an official enquiry by the Earl Marshal in the first few months of 1818. However, according to the Prince Regent, matters had not improved by the time of his mother, Queen Charlotte's funeral in December 1818. After his accession to the throne in 1820, he wrote to the Prime Minister, Lord Liverpool:

> The King desires that Lord Liverpool will acquaint him in the most scrupulous manner, what real power the King has over the Dean and Chapter of Windsor, for a more offensive and troublesome set of individuals to the King personally it is impossible to imagine. This was illustrated by what happened, and which Lord Liverpool cannot forget, their indecent conduct both at the funeral of the King's poor sister Amelia, poor Charlotte, and above all, the King's poor mother.[21]

It is therefore not surprising that, as King, George IV (1820–1830) wished to have little to do with St George's Chapel. The monument erected to commemorate Princess Charlotte, which dominates the Urswick Chantry Chapel (Fig 9.5), was paid for by public subscription, not by the King. The initiative for the monument seems to have come from the sculptor, Matthew Cotes Wyatt, who proposed that members of the public should donate towards a permanent memorial to the much loved and mourned princess. Individual subscriptions were limited to a maximum of one guinea in order to allow as many as possible to contribute. A Cenotaph Committee was set up, under the patronage of the Duchess of York, and over £15,000 was raised for the carving and installation of the monument.

Originally intended for Westminster Abbey or St Paul's Cathedral, the memorial was eventually installed in St George's Chapel in 1824, after some time in storage, to the disquiet of some, who feared that it would not be accessible to the public who had paid for it. However, arrangements were made to grant access to the Chapel and *The Visitants' Guide to Windsor Castle and its Vicinity* (1828), reported that 'The majestic edifice ... was opened for public view in the spring of 1826'.[22]

To allow a clear view of the monument, the sixteenth-century stone screen commemorating Dean Christopher Urswick, which had separated the Urswick Chantry Chapel from the Nave, was removed to the South Quire Aisle and replaced by iron railings. It was not returned until the 1920s.

George IV died in 1830 and was buried in the Royal Vault near his daughter, Princess Charlotte. A reporter for *The Times* noted a lack of respect and grief amongst the public who had gathered in Windsor for the lying-in-state and funeral of George IV; and the new King, William IV (1830–1837), who acted as chief mourner to his brother, was criticised for his behaviour in the Chapel during the funeral, 'talking incessantly and loudly to all about him, so that the most frivolous things were heard'.[23]

Williams IV's behaviour in the Chapel, since George's III's reign referred to as 'the Cathedral', was from thenceforth to be more sober and respectful. He and his Queen Consort, Adelaide, were regular worshippers there, along with members of their households; and, on 21 August 1836, they were accompanied by the widowed Duchess of Kent and her daughter, Princess Alexandrina Victoria, who had been invited to Windsor Castle to celebrate the King's 71st birthday. The Princess recorded the occasion in her journal, saddened by the memory that her father, the Duke of Kent, had been buried at Windsor on his death in 1820:

> The Cathedral made me rather sad. The thought and knowledge that beneath the very stones we were walking on, lay so many near me, in eternal sleep, including my poor dear Father, and that so many more will be placed there, who are now in health and strength, must make one pensive and serious and melancholy.[24]

The birthday celebrations did not go well. William IV allegedly insulted the Duchess of Kent in a speech during his birthday dinner, declaring her unworthy of acting as Regent and expressing his wish to live long enough to avoid a regency. William's wish was granted. He survived just long enough for Princess Alexandrina Victoria to reach the age of eighteen, on 24 May 1837, and thus his niece was able to succeed to the British throne as an adult on the King's death on 20 June that year.

Very little had been done to the fabric of the Chapel since the 'great works' of George III and, whilst George IV and William IV had concentrated on the refurbishment of the Upper Ward and State Apartments, much of the Lower Ward of the Castle, including the Chapel and collegiate buildings, had once more fallen into disrepair. This situation was to change in the reign of Queen Victoria (1837–1901).

Fig 9.8 The east end of the Quire with Benjamin West's window

Fig 10.1 Henry Hobart, Dean 1816–46, portrait by an unknown artist

CHAPTER TEN

Glorification
The Victorian Age

The young Queen Victoria had mixed feelings about taking up residence at Windsor Castle, confiding to her Uncle Leopold in 1837, that Windsor held many sad associations for her. Her reservations were not eased by her attendance at a morning service in St George's Chapel on 27 August 1837, during which she was forced to endure 'a very bad sermon by the Dean'.[25] The Dean in question was Henry Hobart, who had been appointed by the Prince Regent, believing that he was George III's preferred choice, but had been a thorn in his side ever since. After that experience, Queen Victoria chose to worship mainly in the Private Chapel in the State Apartments or the Royal Chapel in the Great Park. Her attendance at St George's in the earlier part of her reign was generally restricted to formal occasions. This no doubt explains her lack of involvement in the major restoration of the Chapel in the 1840s and 1850s.

The 1840s restoration was carried out under the supervision of heraldic artist, Thomas Willement, and was financed largely by the Dean and Canons. Willement was initially employed in 1840 for a limited project, to design and install four new heraldic stained-glass windows in the Quire. In 1841 he was engaged to undertake a much more challenging commission – the restoration of the West Window, which consultant architect Edward Blore had identified as being in a 'perilous state'.[26]

In 1767, Canon Lockman had overseen the resetting and rearrangement of much of the glass in the West Window, interspersing the original panes with coloured glass. By 1841, the eighteenth-century settings were failing and the window was bulging inward. The first task, the removal of the stained-glass panes from the window, was undertaken by stonemason Samuel Cundy and his team, who then went on to repair the stonework mullions. Meanwhile, Willement managed with some difficulty to remove the early-Tudor glass from its eighteenth-century settings and to restore it. He used the opportunity to reorder the figures of Popes, Bishops, Saints, Kings, Knights, armoured soldiers and civilians, to reintroduce ten further figures which had been removed in the eighteenth century and to add six new figures to replace panels in which original glass had been lost. When the glass was reinstalled, the plain eighteenth-century backgrounds were replaced with new coloured glass, decorated with ancient diaper patterns, and the figures were set on plinths under architectural columns and canopies (Fig 10.2).

Willement then supervised a full programme

of works to clean, preserve and beautify St George's and its associated side and chantry chapels, as well as designing and installing a total of twenty-five stained-glass windows in the Quire Clerestory and Quire Aisles. Featuring royal portraits from the College's founder, Edward III, to the late King, William IV, the heraldic windows in the Quire Aisles are a masterpiece of colour, design and heraldic research.

Meanwhile, the organ was restored and re-ornamented, the Quire and Nave vaulting was cleaned and the lime-washing of the eighteenth century was removed to reveal remnants of colour. The Katherine of Aragon window, which had been painted in the eighteenth century to give it the appearance of stone, was revealed to be carved oak. This was stained, varnished and painted with heraldic badges to Willement's designs. The splendid roof-bosses in the Nave and Quire were repainted in bright colours and many of the chantry chapels were reglazed and redecorated, with funds received from descendants of the original founders.

By 1861, when Willement installed his final window, the Chapel had been transformed from an elegant but plain eighteenth-century style into a colourful nineteenth-century decorative scheme, which attempted to recreate the spirit of the Middle Ages. However, the Quire remained dark owing to limited light coming through Benjamin West's painted-glass East Window, which by the mid-nineteenth century was considered by Chapter as 'the acknowledged eye-sore in England's most beautiful Gothic Chapel'.[27]

An opportunity to replace the East Window arose after the tragic death of the Queen's Consort, Prince Albert, in Windsor Castle in December 1861. Wishing to honour the Prince Consort, who had taken a great interest in the Chapel, the Dean and Canons resolved to replace the unfashionable East Window with a new stained-glass window commemorating his life, and to commission a new reredos for the High Altar in his memory. George Gilbert Scott, the leading English Gothic Revival architect of the day, was awarded the commission. Scott was familiar with St George's Chapel. In 1859 he had been chosen by Queen Victoria to design a monument to commemorate her uncle and aunt, the Duke and Duchess of Gloucester, who were buried in a vault beneath in the South Quire Aisle.

Scott employed stained-glass artists Clayton & Bell to design and install the new stained-glass East Window, in consultation with Canon Courtenay, who took a personal interest in the design and iconography. He selected key scenes

Fig 10.2 Detail of West Window figures

Fig 10.3 Gloucester monument in the South Quire Aisle, designed by George Gilbert Scott and sculpted by William Theed the Younger, 1859

from the life of Christ for the higher tiers – the Adoration of the Magi, the Resurrection and Christ in Glory – while the lowest tier depicts 'incidents of public and domestic worth in the life of a prince',[28] commemorating the range of Prince Albert's interests and good works (Figs 10.4-10.5).

Before the stained-glass panes could be introduced in the East Window, Scott had to replace the stonework mullions which had been removed in the eighteenth century. He also fully reinstated the angel-frieze around the window, the side-jambs of which had been removed in the eighteenth century. The frieze was then painted and gilded by Clayton & Bell, who were also employed to gild the magnificent new reredos behind the High Altar (Fig 10.6). The reredos, which had been designed by Scott and sculpted from alabaster by John Birnie Philip and a team of over sixty craftsmen, included further scenes from the life of Christ – the Ascension, Christ meeting Mary Magdalene in the garden after the Resurrection and Christ appearing to the Disciples.

Scott was also responsible for transforming the small chapel to the east of St George's Chapel (on the site of the original Garter Chapel) into a memorial chapel for Prince Albert. Soon after the Prince Consort's death, Dean Wellesley had suggested that this building, then in a largely ruinous state, could be refurbished as an appropriate burial place for Prince Albert. Queen Victoria's decision to construct a new mausoleum in the grounds of Frogmore House therefore disappointed the Dean. Nevertheless, at the suggestion of her daughter Victoria (Vicky), the Crown Princess of Prussia, the Queen agreed to the creation of a memorial chapel on the site. The cost, which amounted to more than £52,000, was met entirely by Queen Victoria from the Privy Purse. The work took thirteen years, from 1862 to 1875.

Fig 10.4 The East Window by Clayton & Bell, 1862–63

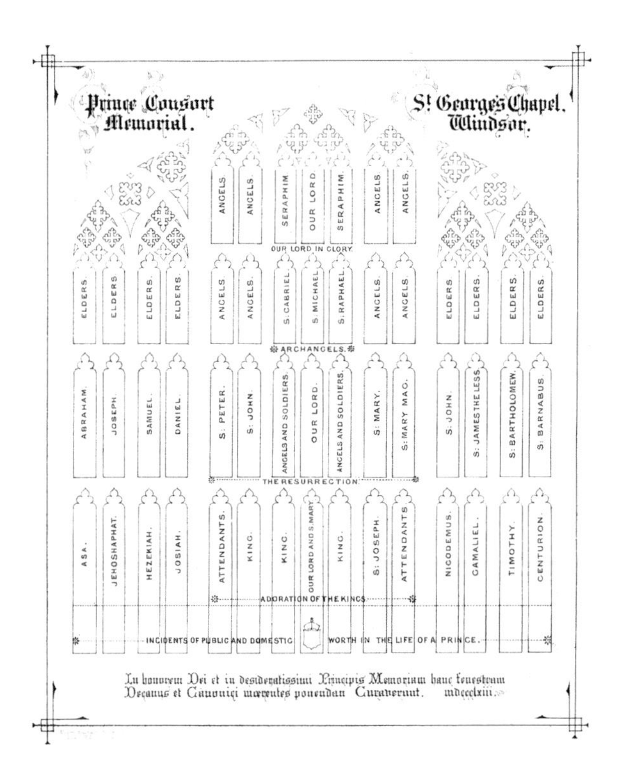

Fig 10.5 Design for the East Window from Canon Courtenay's *The Memorial Window in St George's Chapel*, 1863

Fig 10.6 The alabaster reredos designed by George Gilbert Scott and sculpted by John Birnie Philip, 1862–69

Artists and craftsmen employed on the project included Baron Henry de Triqueti, whose tarsias (decorated marble panels) dominate the walls; Antonio Salviati, whose Venetian workshop produced the mosaics that decorate the vaulting and the west end wall; and Clayton & Bell who were responsible for inserting the mosaics, gilding the vaulting and designing, making and installing the colourful stained-glass windows. The result was spectacular. However, it had not been achieved without problems. Scott, who had been employed by the Queen to supervise the project from its inception, suffered, in his own words, 'a good deal of vexation' from Triqueti, the sculptor engaged by Princess Vicky, who wished to assume artistic control. Relations were so difficult that in 1868, Queen Victoria felt obliged to intervene, instructing another of her daughters, Princess Christian, to ask the Dean to act as peace-maker between the two.

Fig 10.7 Monument to Prince Albert (died 1861) by Henry de Triqueti at the east end of the Albert Memorial Chapel

Triqueti, a French-born sculptor whose work had been admired by Prince Albert, was also responsible for designing and carving the Prince Consort's effigy on the monument at the east end of the Memorial Chapel and the two statues at the west entrance, on which he was still working at the time of his death in 1874. The Albert Chapel was completed and opened to the public at the end of 1875, with two attendants employed to clean the marble and to supervise visitors (up to a maximum of 200 a day by ticket only) and two policemen on duty during opening hours (Wednesday to Friday 12-3pm).

Meanwhile, attention turned back to St George's Chapel, which was being prepared for the marriage of Queen Victoria's eldest son, Albert Edward, to Princess Alexandra of Denmark on 10 March 1863. It was the grandest wedding ever to take place in the Chapel. Elaborately-decorated, although temporary, anterooms were constructed in the Horseshoe Cloister outside the west entrance to the Chapel, to provide accommodation for the preparation of the bridal party, and the Prince of Wales presented himself at the High Altar resplendent in his Garter robes (Fig 10.8).

The recently bereaved Queen witnessed the ceremony from the Royal Closet above the Quire, and hurried back to the State Apartments to greet the newly-weds, insisting on a family photograph beside the bust of the Prince Consort. Six more royal marriages took place in the Chapel during her reign, all faithfully recorded and witnessed by the Queen in the Chapel registers. These were: Princess

Helena with Prince (Frederic) Christian of Schleswig-Holstein in 1866; Princess Louise with the Marquess of Lorne in 1871; Prince Arthur, Duke of Connaught, with Princess Louise of Prussia in 1879; Princess Frederica of Hanover with Baron Alfons von Pawel Rammingen in 1880; Prince Leopold, Duke of Albany, with Princess Helen of Waldeck and Pyrmont in 1882; and Princess Marie Louise, daughter of Prince and Princess Christian of Schleswig-Holstein, with Prince Aribert of Anhalt in 1891.

The royal weddings were to be outnumbered by the numerous royal funerals which took place in the Chapel over Queen Victoria's long reign. These included Princess Mary, Duchess of Gloucester, who died in 1857 and was buried in the Gloucester Vault in the South Quire Aisle, King George V of Hanover, who was buried in the Royal Vault in 1878; and, most significantly, Prince Albert, who was buried in the specially-constructed Frogmore Mausoleum in 1862, after a sojourn in the Royal Vault following his funeral in St George's Chapel in December 1861. Queen Victoria's youngest son, Prince Leopold, Duke of Albany, and one of her grandsons, Prince Albert Victor, Duke of Clarence, both died during her reign and were buried in the Albert Chapel below effigies carved on impressive tomb monuments sculpted respectively by Sir Joseph Edgar Boehm and Sir Alfred Gilbert.

The Queen also commissioned memorials and monuments for friends and relatives buried elsewhere. These included the Prince Imperial (buried in Chislehurst and

Fig 10.8 The marriage of Albert Edward, Prince of Wales, with Princess Alexandra of Denmark in St George's Chapel on 10 March 1863, painting by William Powell Frith

subsequently moved to Farnborough); General Harcourt (buried at Stanton Harcourt, Oxfordshire); Leopold I, King of the Belgians (buried in Laeken, Belgium) and Dean Gerald Wellesley (buried at Stratfield Saye). The monument sculpted by Boehm in memory of her father, Edward, Duke of Kent and Strathearn, was moved from St George's Chapel to the Royal Mausoleum at Frogmore in 1953.

Queen Victoria appointed five Deans of Windsor during her long reign. The second, the Honourable Gerald Valerian Wellesley (Dean 1854–82), nephew of Arthur, 1st Duke of Wellington, became a trusted confidant and friend, supporting her on the death of Prince Albert in 1861 and advising her on Church appointments and other matters. In 1868 he arranged for the installation of a new walkway with iron handrail across the roof from the Deanery, to allow private access for the Queen to the Royal Closet from where she could view services held in the Quire.

On Dean Wellesley's death, in 1882, Queen Victoria was upset that he had chosen the churchyard of Stratfield Saye, where he had served as Rector, for his burial in preference to Windsor. To honour his service as Dean, the Queen commissioned a memorial to him in the North Quire Aisle, with a recumbent figure sculpted from white Carrara marble by Boehm, which she unveiled on 1 December 1884 (Fig 10.11).

Fig 10.9 Gerald Wellesley, Dean 1854-82, portrait by Heinrich von Angeli commissioned by Queen Victoria

Queen Victoria also formed a close relationship with one of her later appointments to the Deanery, Randall Davidson. He had come to her attention in December 1882, when he visited Windsor Castle to report on the death of his father-in-law, Archbishop Tait. The following June she appointed him Dean of Windsor and Domestic Chaplain despite

Fig 10.10 Randall Davidson, Dean 1883–1891, half-length portrait by Rudolph Swaboda, 1890

Fig 10.11 Monument to Gerald Wellesley, Dean 1854–82, by J. E. Boehm in the South Quire Aisle, commissioned by Queen Victoria

his relative youth (he was just 35). Davidson offered personal as well as spiritual support to the Queen, particularly following the death of her youngest son, Prince Leopold, Duke of Albany, in 1884. He also advised her about appointments within the Church of England. As Dean of Windsor (1883–91), he presided over an elderly Chapter and a Chapel in need of structural repair.

Shortage of funds had become a persistent problem for the Dean and Canons after 1867, when an Order in Council, approved by Queen Victoria, enabled the Ecclesiastical Commissioners to appropriate their lands and other properties as part of a national scheme to redistribute the wealth of the Church of England. Prior to this measure, St George's Chapel had ranked as the third-

Fig 10.12 Watercolour by A. Y. Nutt of Horseshoe Cloister from within, looking southwards towards the arch leading to the Parade Ground, 1870. Shows exterior of houses prior to restoration by George Gilbert Scott

richest ecclesiastical establishment in Britain, directly below Westminster Abbey and Canterbury Cathedral, drawing a substantial annual income from the properties granted to them by royal and private benefactors. Compensation was offered, in the form of a one-off contribution of £26,000 to establish a fabric fund and a fixed annual payment of £14,400. Unfortunately the annual income soon proved insufficient and the fabric fund was almost immediately swallowed up in the restoration of the Horseshoe Cloister and the construction of the west steps, both projects completed by George Gilbert Scott in the 1870s.

The broad flight of steps leading to the west door was completed in 1872, replacing a narrow staircase constructed in the early-nineteenth century, which had proved inadequate and even dangerous. The Chapter Clerk recalled that when attending a funeral in 1847 he had 'had a narrow escape from being thrown off the top step'.[29] Scott's west steps continue to provide a distinguished approach to the Chapel on ceremonial occasions such as Garter Day although, due to erosion, the original Victorian stone was replaced with lighter York stone in the 1980s.

In 1874 the Windsor Chapter turned its attention to the Chapel's external stonework, which was showing signs of severe weathering, in particular the decorative grotesques, which were heavily eroded. The London-based firm of Farmer & Brindley was employed to replace them and, between 1875 and 1885, carved and installed at least 239 grotesques on the outside of the Chapel. To fund the external repairs the Dean and Canons managed, with some difficulty, to persuade Parliament to make a grant of £2,000.

A further project, to commission carved figures to occupy the niches on the South Front, was financed by the Knights of the Garter. These Ancaster stone statuettes, also produced by Farmer & Brindley, represented kings and other notable figures associated with the Chapel, including Bishop Beauchamp and Sir Reginald Bray.

Fig 10.13 Ancaster stone statuette of Bishop Beauchamp by Farmer & Brindley, 1880s

Meanwhile, the appearance of cracks in the Nave vaulting was causing concern. In 1883 the Dean and Canons employed architect John Loughborough Pearson to survey the vaulting. On discovering that urgent repairs were needed to prevent its imminent collapse, Pearson was authorized to commission John Thompson of Peterborough to undertake this work at a cost of £2,134. After this major expense, there were no funds left to tackle any repairs to the Quire vaulting. These would have to await the major reconstruction work undertaken by Sir Harold Brakspear in the 1920s.

The funeral of Queen Victoria on 2 February 1901 brought the Queen's association with St George's Chapel to an end. She had died at Osborne, on the Isle of Wight, on 22 January, with the faithful Randall Davidson, a former Dean of Windsor now promoted to Bishop of Winchester, at her side. A few days after her death, Walter Parratt, Organist at St George's Chapel, took some of the Lay Clerks and Choristers from Windsor to Osborne to sing in the Private Chapel there. Bishop Davidson accompanied the Queen's coffin, which was brought over the Solent in the Royal Yacht and conveyed by train to Windsor.

On arrival at Windsor Central station, it was placed on a horse-drawn gun carriage ready to process through the streets of Windsor. However, when the horses took the weight, one of the traces broke, injuring one of the horses, which plunged away from the carriage. With lightning speed, the remaining horses were detached and a group of naval ratings took up the ropes and pulled the carriage through the town to the west steps of the Chapel, a heroic act which saved the day and has been replicated at future royal funerals. Despite the minor delay, the funeral went smoothly in the presence of the Archbishops of Canterbury and York, the Dean, Philip Eliot, and the Bishop of Winchester, Randall Davidson.

Two days later, after a sojourn in the Albert Chapel, the coffin was carried on a horse-drawn carriage, this time without incident, to the Royal Mausoleum at Frogmore, where final prayers were said by Dean Eliot and the former Dean, Bishop Davidson, before the Queen was laid to rest beside her beloved husband, Prince Albert.

Fig 10.14 Queen Victoria's funeral cortège outside the west door of St George's Chapel, 2 February 1901, photograph possibly by J Russell & Sons

CHAPTER ELEVEN

Refurbishment King Edward VII and King George V

On the death of Queen Victoria, the focus of the Royal Court moved from Windsor to London. Although the new King, Edward VII (1901–1910), had been baptised and married in St George's Chapel, he was not a regular attender there. However, he was present at a number of special services to mark royal occasions, including the marriages of Princess Alice of Albany with Prince Alexander of Teck in 1904 and Princess Margaret of Connaught with Prince Gustav Adolph of Sweden the following year. In 1907 King Edward VII gave permission for the Dean and Canons to resume wearing Garter mantles at ceremonies and services connected with the Order of the Garter, a practice which had lapsed under Queen Victoria, who had taken very little interest in the Order.

The King's respect for the Order of the Garter led to his revival of the mediaeval practice of appointing Ladies of the Garter to be present at Garter ceremonies. The first to be appointed was his Queen Consort, Queen Alexandra, in 1901. During his nine-year reign, he appointed twenty-four Knights of the Garter, including fifteen Supernumeraries (Stranger and Royal Knights) who were members of the British or Overseas Royal Families. One of these was King Manoel II of Portugal, who was invested in 1909, and who subsequently came to live in exile in England after a revolution ousted him from the Portuguese throne. However, despite the holding of Garter investitures and related ceremonies at Windsor by King Edward VII, no Garter services or installations took place in the Chapel at Windsor during his reign.

King Edward VII took a close interest in the Military Knights of Windsor. In 1905 he transferred the control of discipline over the Military Knights from the Dean and Canons to the Governor and Constable of Windsor Castle, an intervention which reduced the tension that had built up over the years between them. He encouraged the Military Knights, who remained members of the College of St George, to attend services in the Chapel on a regular basis, and in 1907 he commanded their presence at Sunday Mattins, Obits and other special occasions, reversing a decision made by Queen Victoria to excuse their attendance. He was also responsible for making minor changes to their uniform with the introduction of a white sword-belt.

During the Edwardian period (1901–1910) measures were introduced to enhance the dignity of services in the Chapel. The Dean and Canons wore copes (long cloaks) on a greater number of occasions, the Choir were regularly robed in murrey rather than black, and it became an accepted practice to bow to the High Altar. Holy Communion was celebrated regularly, supplementing the traditional daily services of Sung Mattins (or Morning Prayer) and Evensong (or Evening Prayer).

Dean Eliot introduced a St George's Day service for local Scouts, Church Lads Brigade and Navy League Lads before the First World War. This idea was taken up again after the War and developed into a National Scouts' Service, which has been held almost every year since its inauguration in 1934.

On 6 May 1910, King Edward VII died at Buckingham Palace, in the presence of the former Dean of Windsor, Randall Davidson, who was now Archbishop of Canterbury. The King's body was brought to Windsor and, after a grand funeral in St George's Chapel, was laid to rest in the Royal Vault under the Albert Chapel, whilst a tomb was constructed for him on the south side of the High Altar. Carved by Australian sculptor, Sir Brian Mackennal, King Edward VII's tomb effigy includes his faithful dog, Caesar, who is depicted at the King's feet. It was not until 1927 that the bodies of King Edward VII and Queen Alexandra, who died in 1925, were transferred to the sarcophagus in the South Quire Aisle and a further few years elapsed before the effigy of Queen Alexandra was completed.

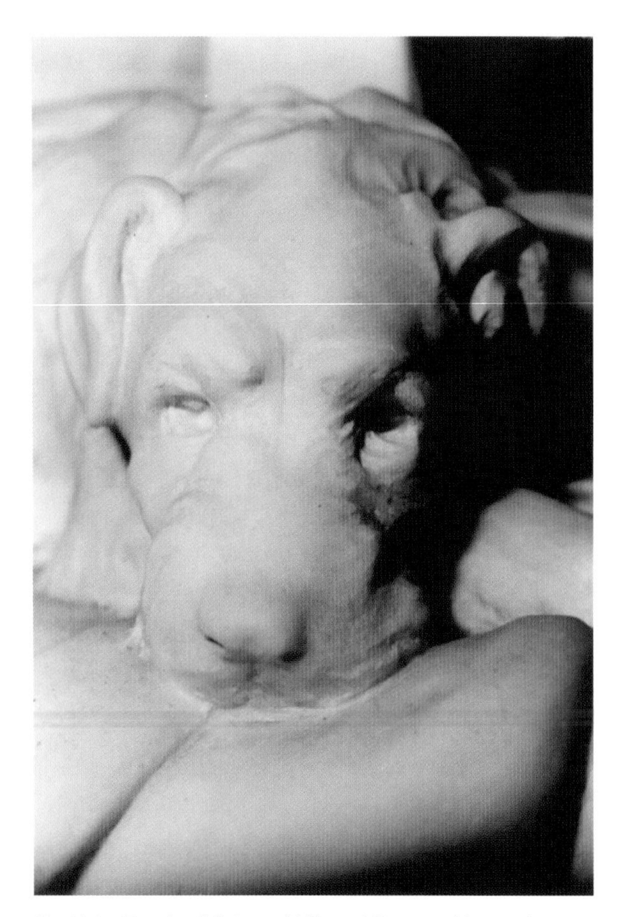

Fig 11.1 Tomb of Edward VII and Queen Alexandra by Bertram Mackennal, 1919, unveiled in 1927. Detail showing Edward VII's dog Caesar at the King's feet

The King's successor, King George V (1910–1936), demonstrated an immediate interest in the Order of the Garter. One of his first actions as Monarch was to command the holding of a Garter Service, which took place on 10 June 1911. He appointed his Queen Consort, Queen Mary, as a Lady of the Garter and she accompanied him in the Garter procession, which made its way on foot from the State Apartments to St George's Chapel for a Service of Thanksgiving. The Prince of Wales (the future King Edward VIII) was invested on this occasion but, although he occupied a stall in the Quire, the service did not include a formal installation ceremony. Similar Garter ceremonies and services took place in the following three years, 1912–1914, until the First World War intervened. The next Garter Service would not be held until 1937.

The outbreak of the First World War in 1914 caused a dilemma for the Order of the Garter. As early as September 1914, *The Times* had been campaigning for the removal of the banners and Garter achievements of the German Kaiser and his family from the Quire, as practised upon earlier Knights of the Garter convicted of treason. King George V hesitated. Many of these Knights were blood-relations. However, in 1915, he reluctantly agreed to the removal of the achievements of eight such Garter Knights (Franz Joseph, Emperor of Austria; William II, German Emperor;

Ernest Augustus, Duke of Brunswick; Prince Henry of Prussia; Ernest Louis, Grand Duke of Hesse; Crown Prince William of Prussia; Charles, Duke of Saxe-Coburg; and King William II of Wurttemberg). Their banners and helms were removed in a private ceremony after Mattins on 14 May. However, the degraded Knights' stall-plates were left in place. This gesture was appreciated by the King's German relations who were entertained in Windsor Castle after the end of the war.

In 1919 a memorial stained-glass window was inserted in the North Nave Aisle listing the former pupils of St George's School who had died in the First World War. Designed and installed by Clayton & Bell, it was funded by the Dean and Canons and the School's Old Boys' Association.

Early in the reign of King George V the poor state of the Chapel building became apparent. Despite the refashioning of parts of the building in the eighteenth and nineteenth centuries, very little structural repair had been undertaken since the days of Sir Christopher Wren, whose 1682 survey report and repair programme had almost certainly saved the Chapel from collapse.

In November 1911, the Chapel's Consulting Architect, Harold Brakspear, and Alfred Young Nutt, the Castle's long-standing Clerk of Works and Chapter Surveyor, proposed major repairs to the Chapel. These were agreed by Chapter in 1913, the year that Nutt retired, but were delayed by the First World War. In 1918, Brakspear commenced a structural survey, which confirmed that the building, in particular the roof structure, was indeed in a perilous state. His 1920 report ended with the words: 'I therefore solemnly warn you that, in my opinion, unless the repairs are undertaken, serious consequences will result and there is a very grave danger of collapse'.[30] The marvel

Fig 11.2 First and Second World War memorial window commemorating former pupils of St George's School, stained glass by Clayton & Bell, 1920–21 & 1949

Fig 11.3a/b Restoration work underway: the south front with scaffolding on the western end (2 photographs)

Fig 11.4 Robert Burns Robertson with craftsmen, including masons and carpenters, involved in the restoration, photographed in 1930

was that the exceptionally wide Tudor vaulting, which rested precariously on thin pilasters, had remained in place for so long. By 1920, the walls had ceased to be vertical and the upper stonework had moved out of alignment leaving the centre unsupported. Urgent repair work was needed to rescue the building. But who would provide the funding?

In 1920, the Dean of Windsor was reluctant to launch a public appeal, since there had only recently been a similar campaign for the restoration of Westminster Abbey. As in the past, the first group to be approached was the Order of the Garter, whose Chapel it was. This appeal raised an initial sum of £25,000; but considerably more was needed. Without financial support from the Church of England, the Dean and Canons were forced to turn to private benefactors. They were fortunate in gaining the services of an excellent fund-raiser, Sydney Walton, whose successful identification of potential donors, particularly 'men who had made money without yet having found a cause to interest them',[31] produced many substantial contributions. Notable among these benefactors was distiller and philanthropist, Lord Woolavington, who alone donated £50,000; the 1st Viscount Cowdray, a contractor who had made a fortune in Mexico; and Frederick Minter, a successful London builder. Minter provided crucial financial stability to the project by agreeing to make up any shortfall in the regular restoration accounts.

Minter's most notable contribution, however, was to finance and arrange for the installation of 'King's Beasts' on the Chapel's pinnacles, to replace those removed on the advice of Sir Christopher Wren in the seventeenth century. The stone statues, which depict mythical creatures associated with royalty, were designed by Brakspear and based on the Tudor statues of royal beasts at Hampton Court. They were carved by sculptor Joseph Armitage in Minter's own building yard in South London. Minter's son, also called Frederick, took a great interest in the work and took over responsibility for overseeing and funding it on the death of his father in 1927. The 'King's Beasts', which perform a structural function as well as a decorative one, dominate the skyline and act as daily reminder of the generosity of the Chapel's benefactors.

Fig 11.5 King's Beasts reinstated on the pinnacles of the Chapel in the 1920s

The restoration programme, which had taken ten years to complete (1920–1930), had cost a total of £175,000. In addition to the external repairs, the interior had been cleaned and the roof-bosses repainted, and a number of other changes and improvements had taken place in various parts of the Chapel. The organ was divided, to allow a full view of the Quire vaulting from the Nave; the sixteenth-century stone screen commemorating Dean Urswick was removed from the South Quire

Fig 11.6 The 1930 Thanksgiving Service to celebrate the reopening of the Chapel after Brakspear's restoration

Fig 11.7 Albert Baillie, Dean 1917–1945, signed painting by Herbert A. Oliver in Deanery

Aisle and returned to its original position in the Urswick Chantry Chapel; and the stained glass in the West Window was rearranged in an order suggested by M. R. James, a renowned mediaeval-art historian who was Provost of Eton at the time.

On 4 November 1930 a Service of Thanksgiving was held in the presence of King George V and Queen Mary and many other members of the Royal Family. It was a splendid occasion attended, amongst others, by the Archbishop of Canterbury, the Prime Minister, the Lord Chancellor and a number of foreign ambassadors. The St George's Chapel Choir was supplemented by the Choirs of the Chapel Royal, Westminster Abbey, Eton, King's College Cambridge and the Cathedrals of Salisbury, Winchester and Christ Church, Oxford.

In the wake of the successful restoration appeal, Dean Baillie recognised the need to set up a building maintenance fund to ensure that resources would be available for future restoration projects. A committee of Knights of the Garter was formed and a fund-raiser, Brigadier General W.G.K. Green, was appointed to make an appeal to the descendants of former Knights of the Garter, who were to be traced by a team of genealogists. Those who responded with donations were incorporated into an association: 'The Association of Descendants of the Knights of the Garter'.

Dean Baillie went on to establish an additional organisation, named 'The Friends of St George's Chapel' to extend the appeal to a wider audience, following the example of the successful society of 'friends' established at Canterbury Cathedral. Founded in 1931 and amalgamated with the Association of Descendants of the Knights of the Garter a few years later, the 'Friends' have supported

Fig 11.8 Travers' College, now part of St George's School, Windsor Castle

Fig 11.9 The tomb of King George V and Queen Mary in the North Nave Aisle

the religious and corporate life and the buildings of St George's ever since.

Further benefactions, notably from Lord Wakefield, Sir Frederick Minter and Miss Violet Wills, enabled the Dean and Canons in 1935 to purchase the site and buildings occupied by St George's School in Datchet Lane. These centred on Travers' College, which had been built to provide alms-houses for the Naval Knights of Windsor in the eighteenth century (Fig 11.8). Travers' foundation was established under the will of Samuel Travers (died 1728), a Windsor worthy and Member of Parliament, to offer accommodation and a living allowance to 'superannuated or disabled lieutenants of English men-of-war'. However, delayed by legal suits, the first appointment was not made until 1795. Less than 100 years later, in 1892, the foundation was abolished, owing to a decline in applications and the increasingly disreputable behaviour of the Naval Knights. Their departure enabled the Dean and Canons to acquire Travers' College, which they had leased from the Admiralty since 1893. Once purchased in 1935, the buildings were adapted, enlarged and improved for school-use. Lord Wakefield then went on to buy the adjacent brewery site as a Silver Jubilee gift for King George V. The King donated it to Chapter and it became a much-appreciated school playground.

In 1935 the Garter Service planned to celebrate the Silver Jubilee was cancelled because of concern about the King's health. He attended the Chapel for a sadder occasion later that year: the funeral of his sister, Princess Victoria, in December 1935. He died soon afterwards at Sandringham on 20 January 1936. After lying in state at Westminster Hall, the King's body was brought by train to Windsor for burial. Following his funeral on 28 January 1936, his coffin remained in the Royal Vault until 27 February 1939 when it was transferred into the sarcophagus in the Nave designed by Sir Edwin Lutyens and sculpted by Sir William Reid Dick. His Queen Consort, Queen Mary, joined him there after her death in 1953.

CHAPTER TWELVE

Renewal
King Edward VIII, King George VI and the Revival of Garter Ceremonies

On the death of King George V in 1936, his eldest son Edward acceded to the throne as King Edward VIII. During his short reign (January-December 1936) he participated in the annual Scouts' Service at St George's Chapel on 19 April 1936 and, on 1 May, he was entertained to lunch by Dean Baillie in the Deanery, after a traditional ceremony in the State Apartments in which the new Monarch received loyal addresses from the 'privileged bodies'. Those delivering loyal addresses included the Dean and Canons of Windsor who, in their address, expressed their delight at his accession and his interest in the Chapel. However, unwilling to end his relationship with a twice-divorced American,

Fig 12.1 King Edward VIII addressing Boy Scouts in Horseshoe Cloister after the Scouts' Service, 1936

Fig 12.2 Interior view of the Quire during the 1937 Garter Service

Mrs Wallis Simpson, who would not have been acceptable as a Queen Consort, Edward VIII abdicated the throne before his Coronation so that he could marry her. Dean Baillie, in a letter to the Friends of St George's Chapel at the beginning of 1937, wrote of his reaction to the Abdication: 'All the hopes with which we began last year have been frustrated. But this time our sadness has in it a note of tragedy'.[32] However, the Dean went on to express his confidence in the uncrowned King's successor, his younger brother Albert, who came to the throne as King George VI (1936–1952): 'We know that he will strive earnestly to carry on the traditions of his father, both in his larger work and in his relation to the Chapel. It argues [*sic*] well that he has immediately decided to hold a Garter Service this year [1937]'.[33]

On 14 June 1937, a Garter Service was indeed held in Windsor, the first since 1914, and was celebrated with full ceremonial, incorporating Garter processions both to and from the Chapel. Six new Garter Knights were installed, including the Earl of Strathmore, the King's father-in-law, and the recently-retired Prime Minister, Stanley Baldwin, who had steered the government firmly but discreetly through the Abdication Crisis.

The next few years were dominated by preparations for the expected hostilities which culminated in the Second World War (1939–1945). On 8 October 1938, Chapter ordered that one hundred gas masks be issued to residents of the Chapel precincts and that foam extinguishers and a sand supply be made available. In February 1939 the Office of Works delivered a report on fire risks to the Chapel and other collegiate buildings and in September that year the Dean and Canons applied to the Ecclesiastical Insurance Ltd to insure the Chapel and domestic buildings against war risks, a request which was initially refused. Preventative measures were taken to protect some of the Chapel's chief treasures. The Garter stall-plates were removed in 1942, at the request of the King, providing an opportunity for a major conservation programme, which continued until 1947; in November 1940 the stained glass was taken out of the West Window to be stored in the Curfew Tower for safety; and the King agreed to fund the costs of protecting the tombs of King George V and King

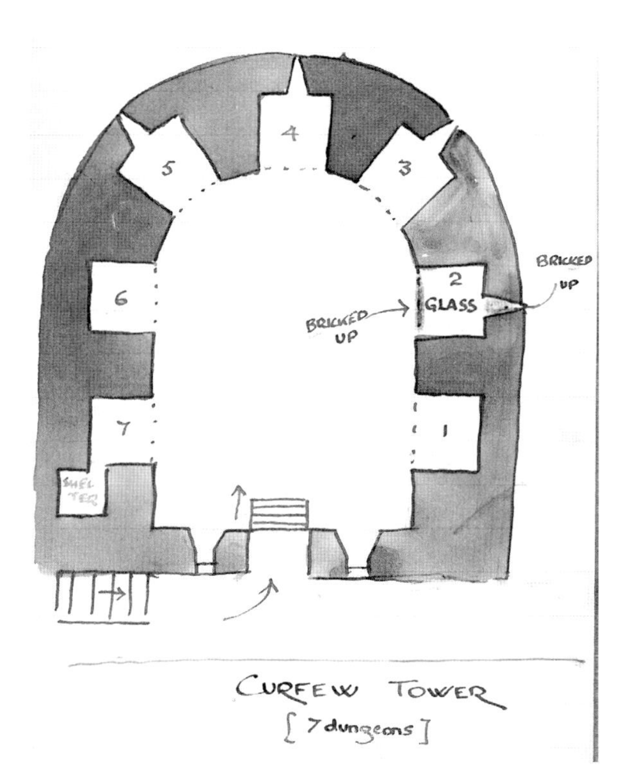

Fig 12.3 Sketched plan by Wilfred Drake of arrangement for storing stained-glass in the Dungeon during the Second Word War

Edward VII and Queen Alexandra as well as the monuments in the Rutland, Beaufort and Lincoln Chapels.

On 2 November 1940 Chapter introduced the following air raid instructions to be observed during services in the Chapel:

> At the sounding of the siren the choir boys will leave the Chapel and go to their air raid shelter at the Choir School. The Lay Clerks will remain; and the music for the rest of the Service will be adapted accordingly … If the "alarm" (danger imminent) signal is received during service time, the prayers will end. All within the Chapel will go to shelter'.[34]

The most significant of the College's books and archives were microfilmed as a security back-up and the Canons were permitted to keep chickens in the Chapter garden. Meanwhile, the Garter achievements of Knights whose nations had become Britain's enemies were discreetly removed, as they had been in the First World War: the King of Italy's on 20 August 1940 and the Emperor of Japan's on 19 December 1941. The Chapel was fortunately spared from war damage, although it had a near escape when a bomb fell on the nearby Great Western Railway Station (now Windsor and Eton Central Station) in October 1940. This no doubt prompted the removal of the stained glass from the West Window and its transfer to safe storage in the Curfew Tower. There it remained until 1945 when the panes were reinstalled by Wilfred Hake.

At 3pm on 8 May 1945, Prime Minister Winston Churchill announced the total and unconditional surrender of Germany. Two hours later a special Service of Thanksgiving was held in St George's Chapel, attended by the Military Knights in uniform and a full congregation. In the years of austerity following the war, Chapter was forced to implement cost-cutting measures, including leaving three of the Lay Clerks' places in the Choir unfilled. This must have made the celebrations for the Sexcentenary of the Order of the Garter in 1948 seem even more magnificent.

On St George's Day, 23 April 1948, King George VI held an investiture ceremony in the Garter Throne Room, followed by a luncheon in the Waterloo Chamber and a procession to the Lower Ward for a Garter Service in St George's Chapel at which the newly-invested Garter Knights were installed. Amongst the fifteen Companions of the Garter invested and installed that day were Queen Elizabeth II, then Princess Elizabeth, and her new husband, Philip, Duke of Edinburgh. A special anthem was written for the occasion by the Chapel's Organist William Henry Harris. Further Sexcentenary celebrations included a festival of music, which took place in the Nave in June, highlighting the music of English composers from the sixteenth century to the present day,

Fig 12.4 Princess Elizabeth and Philip, Duke of Edinburgh, descending the West Steps after their installation at the Garter Service on 23 April 1948

Fig 12.5 The Sovereign's stall and banner in the Quire

and a Service of Thanksgiving for the Order of the Garter, held in St George's Chapel on 18 July 1948, at which Earl Mountbatten of Burma was installed as a Garter Knight.

The renewal of Garter ceremonies at Windsor was so successful that a Garter Service has been held in St George's Chapel almost every year since 1948. King George VI was able to hold two more ceremonies, in April 1950 and April 1951, and in June 1951 he requested that the banners of his deceased predecessors, King Edward VII and King George V, be placed above their tombs in the Chapel. Sadly his own health failed soon afterwards and he died, at Sandringham, on 6 February 1952. After a funeral service at St George's Chapel on 15 February 1952, his coffin was lowered into the Royal Vault where it remained until the completion of the George VI Chapel in 1969. His daughter, who acceded to the throne in 1952 as Queen Elizabeth II and was crowned in 1953, chose to keep her father's Garter banner in place above the Sovereign's stall. It remains now above the stall of King Charles III as a visual reminder of King George's VI's devotion to the Order of the Garter.

CHAPTER THIRTEEN

Stability and development: Queen Elizabeth II and King Charles III

Queen Elizabeth II's association with Windsor Castle spanned nine decades. Prior to her accession to the throne in 1952, Princess Elizabeth enjoyed many childhood visits to Windsor with her sister Princess Margaret, during which they attended services in St George's Chapel on various occasions. Queen Elizabeth II and her Consort, Prince Philip, Duke of Edinburgh, both participated in Garter ceremonies that were held at Windsor almost every year after their installation in 1948, taking part in the grand processions from the State Apartments to St George's Chapel for the annual Garter Service, to the delight of onlookers lining the route.

The Queen attended several marriages in the Chapel, including the wedding of her son Prince Edward and Sophie Rhys-Jones in 1999 and three of her grandchildren: Peter Philips and Autumn Kelly in 2008, Prince Harry and Meghan Markle and Princess Eugenie and Jack Brooksbank in 2018. In 2005 she attended a service of blessing for the marriage of our present King and Queen, then The Prince of Wales and Camilla Parker-Bowles, in St George's Chapel.

In 1959 the Chapel hosted the annual Royal Maundy Service, during which the Queen distributed Maundy money to nominated recipients. The Chapel went on to host the service frequently in the later years of Queen Elizabeth II's reign. On the last occasion, 2022, the Queen was represented at the service by the then Prince of Wales and Duchess of Cornwall. Other special services conducted in

Fig 13.1 Queen Elizabeth II and other members of the Royal Family leave the Deanery with Dean Hamilton on the occasion of the Maundy Service held in Windsor in 1959

Fig 13.2a Queen Elizabeth II distributing Maundy money during the Maundy Service held in Windsor in 2016

Fig 13.2b Maundy purses awaiting distribution, 2016

the presence of Queen Elizabeth II included those commemorating the 50th Jubilee of the Royal Air Force in 1968 and the 660th Anniversary of the College in 2008. The Queen also attended the quadrennial Royal Victorian Order Service at St George's Chapel, the celebration of Easter Day Mattins during the annual Easter Court at Windsor, as well as a number of commemorative concerts and special events. Windsor Castle was a much-favoured residence of Queen Elizabeth II and The Duke of Edinburgh. The Dean of Windsor acted as Royal Chaplain and spiritual adviser during their sojourns here.

More sombre occasions conducted in St George's Chapel include the funerals of the Queen's father, King George VI, in 1952; her uncle, Edward, Duke of Windsor, in 1972; and her sister, Princess Margaret, in 2002; and the interment of her mother, Queen Elizabeth The Queen Mother, in 2002.

In the six decades of Queen Elizabeth II's reign, the College of St George experienced many changes and new developments, whilst never wavering from its central purpose, to offer worship to God and to pray daily for the Sovereign and the Companions past and present of the Order of the Garter. In the twentieth and twenty-first centuries, successful restoration projects and outreach programmes have ensured the future of the magnificent Chapel and College buildings, whilst opening them to an increasingly wide and varied international audience. Generous benefactions and fund-raising initiatives have enabled these developments and helped to maintain daily running of the establishment, including the magnificent Choir, over the years. However, without Crown, State or Church subsidy, there is no room for complacency and the Dean and Canons are well aware that the future of the College depends on continuing financial support from private donors.

Eric Hamilton, who had served King George VI as Dean of Windsor, steered the College through the financial difficulties of the 1950s, introducing admittance charges for tourists and setting up a restoration

Fig 13.3 Eric Hamilton, Dean 1945-62, portrait by Sir Gerald Kelly

appeal in 1958. With the valuable assistance of the Chancellor of the Order of the Garter, Viscount Halifax, and Earl Alexander of Tunis KG, Dean Hamilton was able to raise £120,000 over the next few years to pay for essential repairs to the Chapel fabric and contribute towards the restoration of the Horseshoe Cloister, where the Lay Clerks live with their families. However, the total fell short of the estimated cost of works needed (£199,750), and repairs to the other domestic buildings and other works remained outstanding.

Within the Chapel, Dean Hamilton oversaw a continuing expansion of daily services, initiated a new pattern of worship in Holy Week and introduced new altar rails in the Quire in 1956. Paid for by the Friends of St George's Chapel, they were made of ebonised mahogany and sycamore, inset with painted-glass panels depicting the parables on the Kingdom of Heaven. Dean Hamilton's outreach activities included his visit to Southern Rhodesia (modern Zimbabwe) in 1955 to attend the inauguration of the Central African Province. However, a combination of ill-health and discord within the Windsor Chapter prevented him from achieving all that

Fig 13.4 Design drawing for the George VI Chapel by Seely and Paget

he wished during his ministry at St George's Chapel and, on announcing his forthcoming retirement in the *Annual Report of the Society of Friends of St George's Chapel and the Descendants of the Knights of the Garter* for 1961, he wrote somewhat sadly 'Forgive my shortcomings as your friend and Dean'. He died in the Deanery the following May whilst still in office.

Dean Hamilton's successor, Robin Woods, presided over two major building projects during his nine years in office (1962–1971). One of these, the construction of the George VI Chapel adjacent to the North Quire Aisle, represented (if one excludes the additional buttresses added by Brakspear in the 1920s) the first structural addition to the exterior of the Chapel since 1528. Following the wishes of the late King to be buried underground, in 1967 architect George Pace was commissioned to design a new side-chapel, which was to be completed in stone with lancet windows. The windows were originally intended to be glazed in plain-glass. However, the financial assistance of the Knights of the Garter enabled the employment of John Piper to design a series of elegant, coloured windows, which were made by leading stained-glass artist Patrick Reyntiens.

In 1969 the coffin of King George VI, which had been resting in the Royal Vault since 1952, was transferred to the George VI Chapel to be reburied in a moving private service attended by members of the Royal Family. His widow, Queen Elizabeth The Queen Mother, was to join him after her death in 2002, together with the ashes of their younger daughter, Princess Margaret, who had died earlier in the same year.

The other major building initiative at this time was the reorganisation and conversion of a number of the domestic buildings to create suitable accommodation for a proposed new consultation centre: St George's House. The fruit of the Dean's discussions with Prince

Fig 13.5 Queen Elizabeth II and Dean Woods at the official opening of St George's House in 1966

Philip, Duke of Edinburgh, and others, the centre was intended as a place where 'clergy and laity should work together' to ensure that 'this great Christian foundation shall play a fuller and renewed part in our national life'. St George's House was officially opened by the Queen on 23 October 1966 and continues to hold consultations, which draw participants from many walks of life to discuss an increasingly wide range of topics of national and international significance.

During the building conversion, several mediaeval and early-Tudor wall-paintings were discovered under layers of lime-wash, in numbers 2 and 25 The Cloisters, exciting much interest. Subsequently conserved and cleaned by professional painting restorers, they offer a fascinating insight into the buildings' former occupants. Repair continued on the other College buildings including the fourteenth-century Aerary (treasury), which required reroofing after a major thaw in the winter of 1963–64 caused the roof to leak.

Within the Chapel, Dean Woods inaugurated the Lay Stewards in 1966, a group of volunteers appointed to assist at Sunday services and special occasions such as the Garter Day service, as they continue to do today. As visitor numbers increased in the 1970s these Lay Stewards were supplemented by additional volunteers to fulfil a different but equally important role, to welcome visitors to the Chapel during public opening hours and to offer guided tours and other assistance to the public. From 1973 these volunteers became known as the Voluntary Stewards and in 2002 they were incorporated into a Guild of Stewards. They continue to fill a vital role in the everyday life of the Chapel, alongside the volunteers who man the Chapel shop, arrange the Chapel flowers, repair vestments, assist in the Archives and undertake many other vital duties behind the scenes.

Dean Woods was also involved in the establishment of the annual Windsor Festival of Music and Arts, inspired by a concert in St George's Chapel in 1967 at which Yehudi Menuhin and his sister, Hephzibah, performed. Two years later, with the assistance of Yehudi Menuhin, the first Windsor Festival opened on 17 September 1969 with an outdoor concert in the Lower Ward of Windsor Castle, in

Fig 13.6 Early 16th century wall painting, including St Anthony of Egypt, in No.2 The Cloisters

Fig 13.7 Windsor Festival concert in the Nave, 1969

which the combined bands of the Coldstream and Welsh Guards were conducted by Yehudi Menuhin and William Walton, followed by a fireworks display. Further Festival concerts took place in the Chapel, St George's Hall and the Waterloo Chamber within the State Apartments. The Windsor Festival continues to be an annual fixture in September, with a continually increasing number of activities staged in a wide variety of venues both within the Castle and in the town. Its success has led to the establishment of an additional Spring Festival.

On Dean Woods' appointment as Bishop of Worcester in 1971, Lancelot Fleming was installed as Dean, in the presence of Queen Elizabeth II, The Queen Mother and Princess Margaret. During his time in office, the Garter banner of Emperor Hirohito of Japan, which had been removed from the Quire during the hostilities of the Second World War, was reinstated prior to the Emperor's State Visit to Britain in 1971. Another notable Stranger (Overseas) Knight, Haile Selassie of Ethiopia, took part in the Garter Service at Windsor in 1972. Only three years later his Garter banner was presented to his family after his deposition and murder in his home country in 1975.

1975 also saw celebrations to mark the Quincentenary of the present Chapel, which had been commenced in 1475 by Edward IV. These included a Thanksgiving Service in the Chapel on St George's Day, a lecture on Edward IV by Professor J.R. Lander, concerts and an exhibition in the Vicars' Hall mounted by the Honorary Custodian of the Muniments, Maurice Bond, and his wife, Shelagh Bond who served as the Chapel's Archivist. Dean Lancelot Fleming retired in 1976. In an

Fig 13.8 Garter banner of Akihito, Emperor of Japan, KG with neighbouring banners in the Quire

Fig 13.9 Garter stall plate of Haile Selassie I (1930–1974), Emperor of Ethiopia, KG

obituary following his death in 1990, he was described as 'a retiring gentle man, kind and courteous, in a different mould both from the energetic Dean of Windsor who preceded him [Dean Woods] and the rather politic one who followed him [Dean Mann].'[35]

During his deanship (1976–1989), Michael Mann ran the College with energy and military efficiency, and introduced a number of alterations to the services, including holding Mattins in the Nave. His diplomatic skills were demonstrated in 1988 when he arranged for the remains of Prince Philip's mother, Princess Andrew of Greece, to be transferred from the Royal Vault (where they had lain since 1969) to Jerusalem to be reburied in the church of St Mary Magdalene on the Mount of Olives, as she had wished. Dean Mann was also responsible for presiding over the funeral of the Duchess of Windsor, widow of the Queen's late uncle, before her burial next to the Duke of Windsor at Frogmore. Dean Mann retired in 1989 and, after his death in 2011, his ashes were brought to Windsor to be interred next to his those of his first wife, Jill, in the North Quire Aisle.

Fig 13.10 Dean Fleming inspecting a model produced for the Quincentenary exhibition in 1975

Patrick Mitchell, Dean from 1989 to 1998, was a keen historian and he commissioned an archaeological survey of the Deanery by Tim Tatton-Brown, subsequently securing his employment as Consultant Archaeologist to the Dean and Canons. The Dean promoted and participated in the British Archaeological Association's conference held in the Vicars' Hall in 1998 on the history of Windsor and the Thames Valley, himself contributing a paper on the Garter 'tables' in the Deanery.

He was also behind the establishment in 2001 of a formally-constituted Fabric Advisory Committee (FAC) to succeed the more informal Aesthetic Advisory Committee, which had been formed in 1968 to offer advice on the Chapel buildings and furnishings. Its members included Sir Hugh Casson, who among other achievements was director of architecture for the 1951 Festival of Britain and designed interiors for suites at Buckingham Palace and Windsor Castle. The FAC, which benefits from a range of external expertise meets up to three times a year to discuss matters relating to the Chapel fabric and to offer advice to the Dean and Canons. Recent initiatives approved by Chapter, with the endorsement of the FAC, include stone-cleaning of vaulting within the Chapel, the commissioning of wooden ramps to facilitate access and the introduction of a new sculpture programme for the systematic replacement of eroded grotesques on the exterior.

None of the original grotesques survive, whilst the Victorian carvings that replaced them in the 1870s and 1880s have become worn and disfigured. In a successful collaboration between St George's Chapel and the City and Guilds of London Art School, overseen by the FAC's sculpture group, students were commissioned to design new grotesques for the Chapel. Selected designs were carved in stone and many are now in place on the roof.

The successful grotesques programme was initiated in the time of Dean David Conner, who was installed in 1998. He also oversaw, with the Surveyor of the Fabric, Martin Ashley, an ambitious series of restoration projects on the domestic buildings, funded by external donors, including the refurbishment of no.23 The Cloisters (known as Marbeck), no.8 The Cloisters and much of Canons' Cloister. Dean Conner and his wife, Jayne, endured their

Fig 13.11 Dean Mann at the installation of a new lantern in the Dean's Cloister c.1988

Fig 13.12 Newly installed grotesque on the exterior of the Bray Chantry Chapel, 2006

Fig 13.13 Installing grotesque on the exterior of the Bray Chantry Chapel, 2006

temporary but disruptive relocation from the Deanery whilst the whole building was restored and refurbished from 2013 to 2015.

This ongoing programme of works is supported by the Foundation of the College of St George, established in 2007. The Foundation incorporates the Friends of St George's Chapel and the Descendants of the Knights of the Garter. Now approaching their first century, the Friends and Descendants have grown into a worldwide community of people committed to upholding the values of the College of St George and preserving its magnificent buildings for future generations to enjoy.

In his twenty-five year tenure as Dean, David Conner oversaw significant developments in the administrative structure of the College of St George, working alongside colleagues to ensure the stability and financial security of the Chapel, the School and the House. He also demonstrated great care for the spiritual life and purpose of the College of St George, expressing this in a mission statement that unifies those who live and work there.

> The College of St George is, at its heart, a community of people who live and work together to offer worship to God, prayers for the Sovereign and the Order of the Garter, service to society and hospitality to visitors.

In the early 2000s, both St George's School and St George's House were established as independent companies, but the Dean and Canons of Windsor have remained closely involved in their running as School Governors and members of the Board and Council of St George's House. The working relationship between St George's House and the Dean and Canons had been further strengthened in 1999, when a Canon of Windsor was appointed Warden of the House. Under this structure, the work of the House has flourished and

Fig 13.14 Dean Conner introducing the speaker at the St George's House Annual Lecture, 2023

clearly embodies its founding commitment to contribute to national life.

St George's School has grown far beyond its choir school origins into a 350 pupil, co-educational preparatory and pre-preparatory school that prides itself particularly on the musical opportunities it offers to all of its pupils. In 2011, Dean Conner helped to establish the Queen's Choral Foundation, a charity which supports bursaries for the Choristers to receive education and board at St George's School during their time in the choir.

In 2021, St George's Chapel entered a new period of its history with the appointment of its first female Lay Clerk. In 2022 the first girl choristers joined the choir who sing at services in St George's Chapel daily.

For periods of 2020 and 2021, St George's Chapel had to close to the public in line with the UK Government's national lockdown in response to the Covid-19 pandemic. However, throughout this time, the clergy resident in the Cloisters took it in turns to offer services every day within St George's Chapel. Although they did this alone, they kept the spirit and practice of this community of faith alive. Through The Dragon newsletter, Dean Conner sent weekly messages of comfort and support to the Chapel congregation and friends around the world.

Shortly after the third national lockdown, the nation experienced great sadness at the death of Prince Philip, Duke of Edinburgh. He was aged 99 and had completed 65 years of Royal duties as the Consort of Queen Elizabeth II before retiring as a working Member of the Royal Family in 2017. A Ceremonial Royal Funeral was held for him at St George's Chapel on 17 April. Dean Conner conducted the service and the blessing was pronounced by the Archbishop of Canterbury. Although Covid-19 restrictions were then being gradually lifted, the ceremonial and processional elements of the funeral had to be adapted to accommodate public health legislation. The congregation consisted of just thirty family members, who wore masks and sat in socially-distanced household groups. However, the service in St George's Chapel was conducted in accordance with The Duke of Edinburgh's wishes, including his choice of music, which was performed by a single organist and a choir of three of the Chapel's Lay Clerks and one guest soprano, who, as the wife of another Lay Clerk, was a resident member of the Castle community.

In February 2022, Queen Elizabeth II celebrated her platinum jubilee, marking 70 years on the throne. She was the longest-reigning British monarch, surpassing the record of her great-grandmother Queen Victoria by seven years. Her faithful service to the nation and support for St George's Chapel offered years of peace and stability.

Sadly, her health declined throughout that year and Queen Elizabeth II died peacefully at Balmoral on 8 September 2022. Although many miles away, Windsor immediately became a focus for public mourning with thousands travelling here to pay their respects and lay flowers on the Long Walk even while Windsor Castle and St George's Chapel remained closed during the period of Royal Mourning. On 19 September 2022, following a State Funeral at Westminster Abbey, the late Queen's coffin was brought in procession from London to Windsor, travelling in the State

Fig 13.15 The choir of St George's Chapel on the west steps in 2023

Fig 13.16a The coffin of The Duke of Edinburgh is carried through the nave at his Funeral, 17 April 2021

Hearse along the Long Walk and through the precincts of Windsor Castle to St George's Chapel. A Committal Service was held in the Chapel, conducted by the Dean of Windsor, attended by members of the Royal Family and the Royal Household, foreign royals and many of The late Queen's god children, friends and long-retired personal staff. The service was broadcast live to audiences around the globe. Later that evening the Queen and the Duke of Edinburgh were interred together in the George VI Chapel in a private ceremony attended only by close family and led by the Dean of Windsor.

King Charles III was crowned at Westminster Abbey on 6 May 2023. The following day, a celebratory concert was held at Windsor Castle and the choristers of St George's Chapel made a special appearance to sing alongside Take That in a line-up that also included Katy Perry and Lionel Richie. The King has also continued some of the more traditional connections with St George's Chapel, attending the service of praise,

Fig 13.16b The coffin of Queen Elizabeth II is carried through the nave at the Committal Service, 19 September 2022

Fig 13.17 The Prince of Wales and The Duchess of Cornwall, now King Charles III and Queen Camilla, leaving St George's Chapel after distributing Maundy money, 2022

remembrance and dedication for the Royal Victorian Order and Easter Day Mattins in 2023. The King and Queen Camilla took part in the Garter Day procession and service at Windsor in 2023; King Charles III was appointed a Knight of the Garter in 1958 and installed in 1968 at the age of 19. Queen Camilla was appointed a Lady of the Garter by Queen Elizabeth II and installed in 2022.

On the retirement of Dean Conner in July 2023, the Right Reverend Dr Christopher Cocksworth, Bishop of Coventry, was appointed Dean of Windsor.

Through all the disruption and distractions of recent years, it would be easy to lose sight of the stability offered by the long-standing support of the House of Windsor and the faithful observance of the daily and weekly liturgical round by the Clergy, Choir, Military Knights and other members of the College. In

Fig 13.18 Sung Eucharist in the Quire, 15 June 2017

addition to daily services, which are open to all, outreach activities with local school choirs, interest groups, Chapel visitors, Windsor Castle Learning Centre, visiting choirs and orchestras and many others have encouraged many more members of the public, from near and far, to enter the doors of the Chapel. Once inside, they are able to appreciate fully the aesthetic beauty and the spirituality of this magnificent building, constructed to the glory of God and served faithfully over the centuries by the College founded by Edward III in 1348.

Notes

1. Letters patent of 6 August 1348 quoted in E Ashmole *The Institutions, Laws and Ceremonies of the Most Noble Order of the Garter* (1672) appendix no. I
2. Letters patent of 12 July 1390 quoted in R R Tighe & J E Davis *Annals of Windsor* (1858) I p. 245 n2
3. *Loc.cit.*
4. Contract with William Vertue and John Hylmer for vaulting the Quire, 5 June 1506, quoted in W H St John Hope *Windsor Castle: An Architectural History* (1913) II p. 460
5. John Foxe *Acts and Monuments* (1570) VIII p. 1426
6. SGC XV.58.9*
7. M Gherraerts' description quoted in Roy Strong 'Queen Elizabeth I and the Order of the Garter' *The Archaeological Journal* 119 (1962) pp. 250-1.
8. SGC VI.B.2 136v
9. Extract from A Wood *Athenae Oxonienses* II p. 703 reproduced in *King Charles I: his burial and relics at St George's Chapel, Windsor Castle* (Pitkin 2015) p. 23
10. Lord Clarendon *The History of the Rebellion and Civil Wars in England* (1807) III pt I p.393 reproduced in *King Charles I: his burial and relics* p. 21
11. House of Lords Journal VI p. 30
12. House of Lords Journal VI p. 59
13. W Bray (ed.) *Diary of John Evelyn Esq* (1879) p. 52 quoted in H Vickers *St George's Chapel, Windsor Castle* (2008) p. 50
14. Comment by Thomas Woodcock quoted in G Claydon *The Unlikely Canon* (2009) p. 110
15. Ashmole *The Institutions, Laws and Ceremonies of the Most Noble Order of the Garter* p. 498
16. SGC VI.B.3 f.2
17. Horace Walpole to Miss Berry, 9 October 1791 quoted in P Cunningham (ed.) *The Letters of Horace Walpole, Earl of Orford* (1859) IX pp. 356-7
18. See appendix 2 concerning the Naval Knights
19. C Knight, *Passages of a Working Life during Half a Century* (1864) I, p. 65
20. SGC VI.B.8 Chapter Act, 3 November 1804
21. A Aspinall (ed.), *The Letters of King George IV* III letter 1097
22. C Andrews reported in *The Visitants' Guide to Windsor Castle and its Vicinity* (1828)
23. J Jekyll *The Correspondence of Mr Joseph Jekyll with his sister-in-law, Lady Gertrude Sloan Allaby, 1818–1838* (1894) pp. 242-243
24. Queen Victoria's Journal: RA VIC/MAIN/QVJ (W) 21 August 1836
25. RA VIC/MAIN/QVJ (W) 27 August 1837
26. SGC VI.B.10, 17 May & 22-23 June 1841.
27. SGC XVII.61.20d
28. SGC RBK C.529
29. SGC XVII.9.
30. SGC M.114/3

31 A Baillie *My First Eighty Years, 1864–1944* (1951) p. 181

32 *Annual Report of the Society of Friends of St George's and the Descendants of the Knights of the Garter to 31st December 1936* (1937) p. 5

33 *Loc. cit.*

34 SGC VI.B.14

35 Obituary for Lancelot Fleming by H Vickers, *Daily Telegraph,* 1 August 1990

APPENDIX 1

The Order of the Garter

The Most Noble Order of the Garter, the oldest surviving order of chivalry in the world, was founded by Edward III in about 1348: the precise date is not known. In 1344 Edward III held a magnificent feast at Windsor Castle, at which, according to Adam of Murimuth's chronicle, he declared his intention to establish a round table of three hundred knights 'in the same manner and estate as the Lord Arthur, formerly King of England'. The King ordered the construction of a massive arena in the Upper Ward of the Castle where future gatherings could take place. After the outbreak of war with France and his famous victory at Crécy in 1346, Edward III abandoned this idea, replacing it with a plan for the creation of a smaller, élite brotherhood. It was this body which came to be known as the Company (and subsequently Order) of the Garter, adopting a blue embroidered garter as its emblem. Originally envisaged as a group of twenty-four knights including the Sovereign and Prince of Wales, Edward III decided to increase the total to twenty-six sometime between April 1349 and November 1352. These Garter Knights, who included overseas monarchs and dignitaries as well as English subjects, were chosen in reward for their past loyalty and in the expectation of their future support. Soon after the establishment of the College of St George at Windsor Castle in 1348, St George's Chapel became the spiritual home of the Order, a role which continues today.

The origins of the Order's blue garter and its motto, 'Honi Soit Qui Mal Y Pense' (Shame on Him Who Thinks Evil of It), are uncertain. The popular story, that Edward III coined the phrase when retrieving a garter dropped by a lady of the court (usually thought to be Joan of Kent, Countess of Salisbury), is romantic but doubtful. Another theory, more plausible in the political context of the 1340s, is that the motto refers to Edward III's claim to the throne of France, as the nephew and nearest male relative of the deceased King Charles IV. This claim was to lead to the 'Hundred Years' War' fought by Edward III and his successors against the French.

The number of Garter Knights (also known as Companions of the Order of the Garter) remained twenty-six until 1786, when King George III, wishing all his sons to join the Order, arranged for the Garter Statutes to be altered to allow the appointment of additional (Supernumerary) Knights. These were to include members of the Royal Family, in particular descendants of George I and George II, as well as overseas monarchs and princes (known as Stranger Knights) who had previously been counted within the twenty-six. The composition of the Order was again reviewed in 1954 and now consists of the Sovereign, The Prince of Wales, twenty-four other Companions, and an unlimited number of Royal Companions, who include children and grandchildren of the Sovereign, and of Stranger Knights. They are all appointed by The Queen.

From 1358 to 1488 the Sovereign recruited a number of associated 'Ladies of the Garter' to take part in Garter festivities and ceremonies, although not formally members of the Order. This custom lapsed in the reign of Henry VIII and was not revived until 1901, when King Edward VII awarded the honour to his consort, Queen Alexandra. She was the first of a number of post-mediaeval 'Ladies of the Garter'. In 1987, a statute issued by Queen Elizabeth II permitted women to be appointed full Companions of the Order. Lavinia, Duchess of Norfolk, was the first to enjoy this distinction.

Investiture, the ceremony in which the new Companion is furnished with the Garter ribbon and other insignia including the collar and 'Great George', generally takes place in the Throne Room in Windsor Castle, although it may occur in another royal palace or abroad by delegation. Installation, when the Companion is officially conducted to a Garter stall, can take place only in the Quire of St George's Chapel where the stalls are located. Once assigned a stall, the Knight's sword, helmet and crest (or in the case of a Lady Companion a coronet) are placed on the wooden pinnacle surmounting the stall. A heraldic Garter banner is positioned above it and a brass stall-plate depicting the Companion's coat-of-arms is fixed to the back of the stall. The stall-plate remains in place after the death of the Companion as a permanent memorial, whilst the Garter achievements (sword, crest and helmet or coronet) are removed from the stall and returned to the College of Arms. The Garter banner is offered at the High Altar and, in recent times, has been returned to the deceased Knight's family during a special commemorative service.

Garter feasts and services have been celebrated since the 1340s, principally although not exclusively at Windsor Castle. However, by the beginning of the nineteenth century they were infrequent and in Queen Victoria's reign were allowed to lapse. The twentieth century witnessed a revival. After two special services in 1948 to celebrate the 600th anniversary of the founding of the Order, Garter ceremonies have taken place in Windsor Castle almost every year. Known collectively as the Solemnity of St George, the three-day celebrations and observances include a Garter Feast, a procession to St George's Chapel for a Thanksgiving Service and, on the final day, a Memorial Service for past Companions. Members of the College of St George continue to pray on a daily basis for 'our gracious Sovereign and all the Companions, living and departed, of the Most Honourable and Noble Order of the Garter', according to the wishes of its founder, King Edward III.

APPENDIX 2

The Poor, Military and Naval Knights of Windsor

On the foundation of the College of St George by letters patent in 1348, Edward III included amongst its establishment twenty-four 'poor knights', a number increased to twenty-six in the College Statutes of 1352. The Statutes specified that candidates were to be 'English warriors reduced to great poverty who were to serve God continuously in prayer', attending St George's Chapel daily to pray for the souls of the King and Knights of the Garter. They were to be supported from the revenues of the College, with a daily living allowance of twelve pence (forfeited if absent from the Chapel), forty shillings annually 'for their other needs' and a red cloak with a shield bearing the arms of St George.

Edward III's endowment failed to produce the promised annual income and, in consequence, the Dean and Canons did not appoint the full complement of twenty-six Poor Knights. Before the sixteenth century there were never more than three in post at one time, and frequently only one or two. Henry VIII was determined to redress the situation. His statutes of 1522 reduced the establishment to thirteen, all of whom were to be provided with accommodation within Windsor Castle and with sufficient resources for their sustenance. They were to receive twelve pence a day, as specified in the original College Statutes, and a long gown of white cloth with a shield and cross of St George within the Garter and a mantle of red cloth every year. One of the thirteen was to be appointed Governor, with an additional allowance £3 6s. 8d. each year. To fund the revived establishment, Henry VIII promised to bequeath lands and other properties worth £600 a year to the Dean and Canons in his will. These were indeed conveyed to them by Edward VI and became known collectively as 'the New Dotation'. Edward VI's successor, Mary I, provided a row of accommodation for the Poor Knights, a fact commemorated by the carving of the royal arms of Mary I and her husband, Philip II of Spain, on the Governor's house. The upper houses were adapted from earlier buildings, whilst the lower houses were newly built with stone brought by river from Reading Abbey. Mary I also oversaw the drafting of statutes to govern the establishment and nominated nine of the thirteen Poor Knights, although she did not live long enough to see the appointment of the remaining four or the completion of their accommodation. Final arrangements were left to her sister, Elizabeth I, who issued the new governing statutes in 1559.

There were thirteen Poor Knights until the

mid-seventeenth century, when their number was increased to eighteen by the bequest of Sir Francis Crane, a benefactor who had served as Chancellor of the Order of the Garter and who acted as executor to his brother-in-law, Sir Peter le Maire. Crane combined the £1,500 allocated to charitable purposes in le Maire's will with his own bequest to finance five additional Poor Knights. The new foundation, which became known as the Lower Foundation or Crane's Foundation, was intended to supplement the existing establishment, which thenceforth became known as the Upper or Royal Foundation. Sir Francis Crane died in 1636. However, a series of protracted law-suits concerning the terms of his will, delayed the establishment of the new foundation until the 1650s. A block of almshouses, known as Crane's Building, was constructed to accommodate the additional knights. It stood against the west wall of the Castle until its demolition in 1847. The site is now occupied by a Victorian guard house, built in 1863.

The Poor Knights survived the occupation of Windsor Castle by Parliamentary troops during the Civil War and Commonwealth, despite the dissolution of the College of St George. However, the ejection of the Dean and Canons from the Castle in 1643 and the confiscation of their lands and other assets left the Poor Knights without a source of income. They petitioned for financial assistance, describing themselves in the petition as 'so many old decayed Gentlemen who have spent the best part of our lives in the service of our country'. Somehow they managed to survive this situation, despite the occupation of many of their houses by royalist prisoners, whilst Oliver Cromwell set up a commission to inquire into the terms of their foundation. Satisfied that they were fulfilling their founder's intentions, Cromwell issued ordinances 'for the continuance and maintenance of the Poor Knights' in 1654, endowing them with income from some of the Dean and Canons' former properties. The Poor Knights were present at Cromwell's funeral in Westminster Abbey in 1658.

Shortly after the Restoration of the Monarchy in 1660, Charles II issued an order that the Poor Knights of the Lower Foundation were to enjoy the same privileges as the Upper Foundation. However, the former continued to seek promotion to the Upper Foundation when vacancies arose. In the early-twentieth century, the Lower Foundation was abolished, restoring the total number to thirteen.

In 1833 William IV renamed them the Military Knights of Windsor, primarily to raise their status in line with the more recently established Naval Knights of Windsor. The latter had been founded under the will of Samuel Travers, a Windsor worthy and Member of Parliament, who had died in 1728. Following lengthy legal disputes over the will, the first nominations of the 'superannuated or disabled lieutenants of English men-of-war' took place in 1795. However, it was not until 1803 that the full complement of 'Poor Knights of the Foundation of Samuel Travers' was installed in St George's Chapel. They soon became known as the Naval Knights of Windsor and adopted a uniform consisting of an embroidered blue coat with white facings and with white breeches. This prompted William IV to assign to the Military Knights a military uniform to replace the plain cloaks worn previously. Representing the uniform adopted by those unattached to any regiment, this uniform is still worn by the Military Knights on formal occasions, albeit with the addition of a white belt.

The Naval Knights' establishment lasted less than one hundred years. In 1892 it was dissolved due to falling applications, poor attendance and disreputable behaviour. The remaining Naval Knights were reluctant to resign their pensions and to leave Travers'

College, the building constructed for them in the eighteenth century at the foot of the Castle walls. Three departed under protest, whilst the last one, Governor Willis, was forcefully evicted on 20 January 1893.

The Military Knights continue to live in the houses provided for them in the Tudor period. They regularly attend services in St George's Chapel, wearing uniform and processing on Sundays during College terms and at special services, such as the Garter Day service and the quarterly Obits. Several changes have taken place over the years, including the transfer of disciplinary matters to the Governor of Windsor Castle in 1905. Military Knights are now required on appointment to be married, reversing the original regulation that they should be unmarried or widowed. Most have duties within the Military Knights' establishment as well as assisting voluntarily in the smooth running of the College of St George, of which they form a unique and important part.

APPENDIX 3

The Musical Establishment

The College of St George has possessed a choir since its foundation in 1348. The first College Statutes, issued in 1352, specified the appointment of four Clerks (singing-men) and six Choristers as well as twelve Priest-Vicars, who between them were responsible for singing the daily round of eight services of Divine Office (Mattins, Lauds, Prime, Terce, Sext, None, Vespers and Compline) and several daily celebrations of the Mass. According to the Statutes, the liturgy was to be sung in 'its proper chant as is accustomed to be done in cathedral churches' and services to be conducted following 'the Sarum use' (the form used in Salisbury Cathedral). Soon after its foundation, the Choir supplemented the plainsong chants with settings of texts in three-part or four-part harmony, known as polyphony. This development was almost certainly promoted by John Aleyn (Canon of Windsor 1362-73), himself a composer, who at his death in 1373 bequeathed a roll of polyphonic music to St George's. Canon Thomas Dannet or Damet (Canon 1431-1436); Canon Nicholas Sturgeon (Canon 1441-1454) and Walter Lambe (Master of the Choristers 1479-1484) also composed for the Choir. All three were contributors to a missal known as 'The Old Hall Manuscript', which survives in the British Library (Additional MS 57950) and is considered to be the best extant source for late medieval sacred English music

The musical establishment grew in size after the construction of the new St George's Chapel by Edward IV, commenced in 1475. At the time of Edward IV's death, in 1483, the east end was essentially complete. Services were transferred at about this time to the newly-finished Quire, which provided a magnificent setting for the worship of God in words and music. As part of his ambitious plans for the new Chapel, Edward IV ordered the Choir to be strengthened, with the addition of more boys and professional singing men. After some difficulty recruiting sufficient qualified musicians, the Choir reached its full capacity by Christmas 1482, comprising sixteen Vicars, one Gospeller and two Epistolers (who between them read or chanted the Gospel and Epistles from the Holy Bible), thirteen Lay Clerks and thirteen Choristers. The Horseshoe Cloister, a handsome set of twenty-one lodgings, was constructed at the west-end of the Chapel at this time, to provide accommodation for the expanded establishment. The houses continue to be occupied by Lay Clerks and Chapel staff today.

For more than 675 years, with the exception of a brief interval in the seventeenth century, the Choir has played a key role in the worship of God within the Chapel, producing music of exceptional quality. It has benefited from the talents of a succession of leading professional musicians who have served as Organists, Masters of the Choristers and Directors of Music. John Marbeck, perhaps the most famous of these, held office as Organist from c.1531 to c.1585. Marbeck, a distinguished theologian as well as a musician and composer, narrowly escaped death after his conviction for heresy in 1543 for his Protestant views. Fellow St George's musician, Robert Testwood, was convicted alongside him and was burned with two other Windsor residents. However, Marbeck won a reprise and was thus saved from becoming one of 'The Windsor Martyrs'. He went on to compose a musical setting for the words of the Book of Common Prayer in English, which had been introduced in 1549 by Edward VI. His setting, The Booke of Common Praier noted, published in 1550, is still in regular use in the Chapel today. His theological works included the first concordance of the English Bible, which he dedicated to Edward VI, describing himself in the preface as 'altogether brought up in your highnes College at Wyndesore, in the study of Musike and playing on Organs'. Although the use of organs was subsequently banned under the Protestant regime of the Lord Protectors Somerset and Northumberland, Edward VI granted that Marbeck and his fellow Organist, George Thaxton, should be paid 'in as large and ample maner as if organ plaing had still continued in the Churche' in injunctions issued in 1551.

Other talented musicians who served St George's Chapel during the sixteenth and seventeenth centuries included Richard Farrant (Organist 1564-1580), John Mundy (Organist c.1580-1630), Nathaniel Giles (Master of the Choristers 1585-1633) and William Child (Organist and Master of the Choristers 1632-1643 and 1660-1697). They were responsible not only for producing a high standard of music in the Chapel but also for recruitment to the Choir. In Elizabeth I's reign, Farrant was paid for riding about the country to secure skilled boys, making use of a writ of impressment, which the Queen had issued to the College on 8 March 1560, allowing them 'to take as many of the most cunning singing men and boys from any place within this Realm' with the exception of the Chapel Royal and St Paul's Cathedral. She declared her wish to maintain and enhance the excellent reputation that the Choir had acquired in the reign of her father, Henry VIII.

Despite the disruption of the English Civil War and Commonwealth, when the St George's Chapel Clergy and Choir were ejected from the Castle (1643-1660), William Child managed to revive and enhance the reputation of the Choir after the re-establishment of the College in 1660. Samuel Pepys was impressed by a service he attended in the Chapel on 26 February 1666 and recorded in his diary: 'it is a noble place indeed and a good Quire of voices'.

The practice of employing talented musicians to direct the Choir has continued, with a succession of Organists and Directors of Music keeping alive the best of English cathedral music, some of which has been composed specifically for St George's Chapel. Walter Parratt (Organist 1882-1924), Sir Henry Walford Davies (Organist 1927-1932), William Henry Harris (Organist 1933-1961) and Sidney Campbell (Organist 1961-1974) contributed music to the Choir's repertoire which is still in use today. The Choir currently comprises twelve Lay Clerks and (at full capacity) twenty-four Choristers, including trainees known as probationers. It plays a central part in the worship of God in the Chapel, maintaining the level of musical excellence envisaged by the College's founder, as well as performing in concerts and other musical events. Until the twenty-first century, it was an exclusively male-voice choir, but in 2021 the Dean and Canons appointed the first female Lay Clerk and the first girl choristers in 2021 and 2022 respectively. A setting of the words of the Collect of St George was commissioned by composer Joanna Marsh to mark this.

Throughout its long history, the musical establishment has been the financial responsibility of the Dean and Canons, who have provided accommodation, training and subsistence to the Organist and Choir, as well as education for the Choristers. For many years, it has represented the largest single cost in the annual running expenses of the College, depending on the generosity of benefactors for its survival. In 2012 the Queen's Choral Foundation was established as a formal focus for fund raising. The future of the Choir rests on its success.

APPENDIX 4

St George's School, Windsor Castle

St George's School has its origins in the instruction provided to the medieval Choristers of St George's Chapel. From its foundation in 1348, the College included Choristers to take part in daily worship. The College Statutes of 1352 specified that six Choristers be instructed in the three aspects employed in the daily services – text, chant and ceremony – and that one of the Priest Vicars 'more learned than the rest in teaching grammar and singing' be appointed as 'Grammar Master' to teach the boys. Instruction was to be taken seriously and, if necessary, the boys were to be excused from services to attend their lessons. Collectively they formed one of a number of song-schools established by cathedrals and colleges at this time, which offered aspects of the wider curriculum available in grammar schools as well as liturgical instruction. According to the Statutes, the boys were to remain in the Choir 'for the time only during which they were endued with fulness of voice'.

In the fifteenth century, Edward IV reconstituted the College on a grander scale, with a new Chapel building and a larger Choir, including thirteen Choristers. To cope with the increased number of boys and with the growing complexity of the music, the duties of the Grammar Master were divided between two members of the clergy. The 'Instructor of the Choristers', or 'Master of the Boys', was to teach liturgy and associated skills, whilst the newly appointed 'Supervisor of the Choristers' was to take care of domestic and financial matters. The Masters were also to ensure the recruitment of sufficient Choristers, a task made increasingly difficult by the shortage of suitable candidates and the poaching of trained choristers by rival establishments. They were allocated travel expenses for riding round the country not only to recruit new boys but also to search for and bring back missing Choristers.

Until the nineteenth century, the Choristers lived within the Chapel precincts. Originally, they probably lodged with the Priest Vicars. The College accounts for 1459–1460 record payment for repairs carried out in 'the house of the vicars and choristers'. In addition they needed a place to learn and rehearse. The remnants of painted musical notation on the walls of a room in no. 25 The Cloisters indicate that this was the schoolroom used for teaching Choristers in the late-fifteenth century. Christopher Urswick (Canon 1492–96; Dean 1496–1505) considered the provision for the Choristers inadequate. Whilst Dean, he ordered the repair of 'the house in which they sometime live'. When a chantry was established for him at Windsor in 1507, the Dean and Canons instructed the Choristers to say daily prayers for Urswick and directed that seven pence be distributed to each boy annually to pay for ink and paper for writing practice in accordance with Urswick's wishes. Richard III contributed further to the well-being of the Master and Choristers in 1484 by granting an annual gift of thirteen cartloads of firewood from Cambourn Forest.

However, the accommodation of the Choristers remained inadequate and there was nowhere within the College set aside for their meals or recreation, leading them to eat and drink in the town. Believing this to be 'to the great dishonour of the college', James Denton (Canon 1509–1533) ordered the construction, at his own expense, of a building in the Lower Ward where the Choristers and Chantry Priests could live and eat. The building, which was completed in 1519, became known as Denton's Commons. The following year Canon Denton drew up a comprehensive set of regulations to govern its occupants, including the requirement that one of the boys should daily read from the scripture at mealtimes and that the Master of the Choristers should reside permanently in the commons to ensure the boys were cared for and behaved themselves. Sadly the early-sixteenth century building was demolished in 1859.

The Choristers were amongst other members of the College ejected from Windsor Castle in 1643 during the English Civil War. On the return of the Dean and Canons to Windsor after the Restoration of the Monarchy in 1660, one of their first tasks was to re-establish a choir. Organist William Child returned to Windsor to resume his duties, and a new Master of the Boys was appointed to oversee the recruitment and management of the Choristers. Gradually the Choir reached its pre-war strength and has continued its role in the daily worship in the Chapel to the present day. During this time, the boys have been accommodated in a number of different places within the Castle walls, including Denton's Commons (until its demolition in 1859) and in a Choristers' house in the Horseshoe Cloister. In 1893 a major change took place when the Dean and Canons acquired a lease on Travers' College, the building previously occupied by the Naval Knights of Windsor, and adapted it to house the school.

The move to Travers' College enabled a significant expansion in the number of pupils, who now included non-choristers (who became known as 'supernumeraries' or 'supers'), and the broadening of the curriculum. Further developments were the introduction of choral scholarships, the refurbishment of Travers' College after it had been purchased from the Admiralty in the 1930s, the acquisition of the neighbouring brewery site in 1936, the addition of a pre-preparatory department and the introduction of girl pupils in 1996. The choir school, which was renamed 'St George's School, Windsor Castle' on its move to Travers' College in the 1890s, continues to flourish, combining its traditional role – the accommodation and instruction of choristers – with the provision of a broad-based modern education enjoyed by a wider range of pupils. Part of the College of St George, the school includes the Dean and Canons on its board of governors. On a daily basis, during term-time, the Choristers climb the steps from the school to the Canons' Cloister and proceed to the 'song-school' on the north side of the Chapel. The practice room forms part of house known as 'Marbeck', named in tribute to former organist and composer John Marbeck. On entering the precincts in the morning, it is a delight to hear the sound of Choristers rehearsing for the Chapel, which they have served generation by generation for more than 675 years.

APPENDIX 5

St George's House

On 23 October 1966, after a service of thanksgiving and dedication in St George's Chapel, Queen Elizabeth II officially opened St George's House. Occupying two refurbished seventeenth-century Canons' houses, this new residential consultation centre was intended to accommodate groups of delegates (both clergy and laity) to enable them to explore and discuss matters of mutual interest and importance. The idea for establishing the House originated with Dean Robin Woods. Soon after his appointment to the Deanery of Windsor in 1962, he became convinced that the College of St George was in need of major reorganisation and renewal in order to restore its financial stability, to preserve its historic buildings and, in particular, to ensure its continuing relevance to the outside world. His previous experience as Chairman of the Industrial Mission, and as a senior army chaplain, had convinced him of the value of dialogue between clergy and laity on matters affecting modern life, and of the benefits of in-service leadership training, which he hoped could be extended to senior clergy. The establishment of a consultation centre within Windsor Castle would offer a way of promoting both these initiatives, whilst also providing an opportunity to obtain funding to renovate some of the College's historic buildings. In developing such a vision, he benefited from the encouragement, support and advice of Prince Philip, Duke of Edinburgh, who shared Dean Woods' views on the importance of training and dialogue.

A successful series of financial appeals resulted in sufficient funds to convert and renovate the two houses which would form the main residential accommodation, nos. 9 and 10 The Cloisters, whilst also permitting the modernisation of nine other houses in the Canons' Cloister and Denton's Commons and the refurbishment of the Chapter Library. They also enabled the establishment of a reserve fund which would be needed to administer St George's House until it became financially self-supporting. By 1968 all the building works were complete and the House had reached full staffing-levels with the appointment of a Director of Studies in addition to the Warden and Bursar who had been in post from the outset. The first senior clergy course took place from 30 September to 7 October 1968 and the first mid-service clergy course in 1969. In 1968 a series of consultations on business ethics commenced, attended by industrialists and trade-union members. Interfaith gatherings also became a regular feature of the St George's House programme.

The House's current consultation programme focuses on three distinct areas: contemporary issues, service to the Church and external consultations which fall within the core objectives of the House. The annual programme is varied, rich and intellectually challenging. In 2016, a number of events took place to mark the fiftieth anniversary of the founding of the House. As part of the celebrations, a Society of Leadership Fellows was established to encourage leaders from various walks of life to meet and share their experience and wisdom.

Deans of Windsor

John de la Chambre, 1348–49
William Mugge, 1349–81
Walter Almaly, 1381–89
Thomas Butler, 1389–1402
Richard Kingston, 1402–18
John Arundel, 1419–54
Thomas Manning, 1454–61
John Faulkes, 1461–71
William Morland, 1471
John Davyson, 1471–73
William Dudley, 1473–76
Peter Courtenay, 1476–78
Richard Beauchamp, 1478–81
Thomas Danett, 1481–83
William Beverley, 1483–85
William Morgan, 1485–96
Christopher Urswick, 1496–1505
Christopher Bainbridge, 1505–07
Thomas Hobbs, 1507–09
Nicholas West, 1509–15
John Voysey alias Harman, 1515–19
John Clerk, 1519–23
Richard Sampson, 1523–36
William Franklain, 1536–54
Owen Oglethorpe, 1554–56
Hugh Weston, 1556–57
John Boxall, 1558–60
George Carew, 1560–71
William Day, 1572–96
Robert Bennett, 1596–1603
Giles Tomson, 1603–12
Anthony Maxey, 1612–18
Mark Antony de Dominis, 1618–22
Henry Beaumont, 1622–27
Matthew Wren, 1627–35
Christopher Wren, 1635–59
Edward Hyde, 1659 (not installed)
Bruno Ryves, 1660–77
John Durell, 1677–83
Francis Turner, 1683–84
Gregory Hascard, 1684–1708
Thomas Manningham, 1709
John Robinson, 1709–14
George Verney, 12th Baron Willoughby de Broke, 1714–28
Peniston Booth, 1729–65
Frederick Keppel, 1765–77
John Harley, 1778–87
John Douglas, 1788–91
James, Earl Cornwallis, 1791–94
Charles Manners-Sutton, 1794–1805
Edward Legge, 1805–16
Henry Lewis Hobart, 1816–46
George Neville Grenville, 1846–54

Gerald Wellesley, 1854–82
George Henry Connor, 1882–83
Randall Thomas Davidson, 1883–91
Philip Frank Eliot, 1891–1917
Albert Victor Baillie, 1917–45
Eric Hamilton, 1945–62
Robert Wylmer Woods, 1962–71
Launcelot Fleming, 1971–76
Michael Mann 1976–89
Patrick Mitchell, 1989–97
David Conner, 1998–2023
Christopher Cocksworth, 2023–

Index